INTRIGUING INDIA
THE VIBRANT
West

INTRIGUING INDIA
THE VIBRANT
West

HUGH AND COLLEEN GANTZER

NIYOGI
BOOKS

Published by

NIYOGI BOOKS
D-78, Okhla Industrial Area, Phase-I
New Delhi-110 020, India
Tel: 91-11-26816301, 49327000
Fax: 91-11-26810483, 26813830
email: niyogibooks@gmail.com
www.niyogibooks.com

Editor: Gita Rajan
Design: Write Media

ISBN: 978-93-81523-10-0
Year of Publication: 2012

Printed at: Niyogi Offset Pvt. Ltd., New Delhi, India

Contents

The legendary gate to the Gadisar, Jaisalmer.

Preface

The sea defines our West.

Wave after wave of traders, adventurers and would-be conquerors, left the squalor of their crowded homes and trimmed their sails for legendary India. They had heard of the wealth and wisdom of its people, and of its great resources and had wanted their share of this intriguing land. We saw their footprints on the sands of the Arabian Sea, traced the strands of their principles and prejudices woven into the mores of our people, admired their architectural conceits imprinted across our landscape.

Eventually, India conquered them all. Though a few misguided souls tried to uproot evidence of their historic presence, these were the brief burps of indigestion created by short-lived, self-serving, demagogues. The traditional tolerance of Indian society prevailed. We are not a nation of Traders, but of Learners and Adapters. Drawing on our ever-increasing reservoir of cultural genes we do not attempt to reinvent the wheel. Instead, like a swiftly-evolving organism, our society constantly exchanges cultural DNA from its ethnic matrix to meet new challenges.

In our travels across our western states we have experienced:

- The great ruins of a cryptic civilisation which flourished in the saline plains of Gujarat in 2,600 BC, created miracles of conservation and furnace-based technology; and as mysteriously, vanished.
- A Stone-age gallery of rock art that could have predated the emergence of man from the Rift Valley of Africa.
- The incredible resilience of a small community of Zoroastrians who fled persecution in Iran, centuries ago, and have continued to preserve their faith while adding immeasurably to India's stature.
- The radiant saga of a Muslim mystic whose Hindu devotees have erected a great, and growing, town dedicated to the welfare of all who need help.
- A grass-roots organisation of lunch transporters whose time-bound delivery system ranks with that of the best corporate houses in the world.
- A predominantly Hindu state with a town of ancient Portuguese churches revering the uncorrupted body of a Christian saint and exploding with the uninhibited festivities of a pre-Lenten Carnival.

Interceders at the glittering tomb of a princess, Ajmer.

All this has been achieved in a land in which four world-spanning faiths have been born and every other global religion thrives, along with innumerable sects, cults and eclectic variations of beliefs. We are not a spiritual nation. We are a nation that seeks new frontiers of spiritual development with the same dedication that we seek the good life.

Out of this seeming conflict of aspirations has been born the endlessly Intriguing India that we have seen, touched, heard, felt and tasted during our voyages across our incredibly varied land.

This is the excitement which drove this book.

India's First City – 2,600 BC

DHOLAVIRA

The gerbils greeted us.

They popped up, stared at us goggle-eyed, squeaked, ducked back into their burrows. They had colonised Dholavira long before people had. But we don't know who those people were. Four thousand, six hundred, years ago, in Gujarat's Rann of Kachch, an unknown race had built a wondrous city atop a hillock at the edge of the sea. Then they had abandoned it and now only the gerbils remained, tunnelling their burrows in the sands at the base of the mound that had grown over the hidden city.

In 1967, Jagatpati Joshi discovered that scrubby mound for the Archaeological Survey of India. Very slowly, very carefully, the well-preserved ruins of the city began to appear. It was, clearly, part of the ancient Harappan, also known as the Indus Valley Civilisation.

Early one morning in March, we stood in the scanty shade of a thorn tree and looked across a dusty stretch, pock-marked with gerbil burrows, at the impressive rise of Dholavira. Massive brick walls soared in receding terraces to a high citadel. Deep, water-harvesting, reservoirs encircled the base of this ancient metropolis.

One of the many reservoirs of Dholavira.

"The Museum map showed only a few reservoirs," said a local man who had attached himself to us as we strolled around the interesting Archaeological Museum, built just outside the perimeter fence of the hulking ruins. One of his companions had claimed that his grandfather, retired postmaster, Shambudan Gadhvia, was the real discoverer of Dholavira. "He had always known that there was something special about the mound and he had alerted the government. But they've all forgotten him."

Now, under the thorn tree, our self-appointed guide said, "There were really sixteen reservoirs. This is why it was called *Dhola Vira*, the White Brother. Our women refer to wells as 'brothers' because they help them survive in this dry land. We get only 300 to 400 mm of rain, and it all comes over a very short period, filling the *nullahs*. Then the land dries."

He led us across one of the two shallow ravines that become raging torrents when it rains in the distant hills. It was then that we began to discover the achievements of the ancient Dholavirans. Using check-dams, they had diverted the water of the torrents into enormous, brick-lined, reservoirs. "Their fired bricks are wedge-shaped so they fit tightly into each other making the reservoirs water-tight even to this day, four thousand, six hundred years later." We looked down at those deep, wide, tanks, abandoned and dry now. They had steps going down to the bottom, predecessors of the elaborate step-wells of Gujarat. In our mind's eye we saw long lines of slim women walking up and down the steps of the reservoirs, balancing pots of water on their heads.

We clambered up to the equivalent of the Nob Hill of Dholavira: the so-called Citadel. This is a misleading term normally applied to a fortress overlooking or protecting a city. In fact this 'Citadel' was where the leaders lived, sequestered by thick stone walls and gates. It was a 'gated community'. Some scholars believe that the privileged people

Walled tiers rising to the Citadel.

who resided here were priest-kings like those in the Sumeria of that age. But there are no ruins of temples or the remains of impressive sacred statues indicating a powerful theocracy. We believe that Dholaviran society was a technocracy, the first of its kind in history. The Citadel was where the CMD, CEO, COO and other honchos lived. There is, also, an undeciphered signboard of 10 characters which could have stood here. We believe that this, the world's first street sign, permitted the entry of hand-pulled hawkers' carts carrying domestic ware and fresh supplies, but prohibited animal-drawn heavier vehicles.

In many of our exclusive gated communities, today, noisy heavy vehicles are not allowed to disturb the peace of their privileged residents.

These protected technocrats oversaw the craft units working in the 'Baileys' on the next level, immediately below the 'Citadel'. The 'Baileys' were the creative centres of this great complex. Here craftsmen and artisans produced jewellery out of sea-shells and semi-precious stones with some of the beads so finely drilled that nothing thicker than a human hair could pass through. They also carved signets on soapstone. Traders used these to impress their trademarks on clay seals to identify their goods. From the smoky smelteries and forges of the lower town came copper to be fashioned into ornaments and implements. The skilled technicians of the Citadel also oversaw the clay-workers and potters of the lower town who probably created the small votive figurines for family shrines and well made jars and other pottery. According to archaeologist Dr. P. Ajithprasad, "There existed an elaborate network of sites primarily meant for resource management and distribution of finished craft products."

Women workers are dwarfed by India's first SEZ, circa 2,600 BC.

The walls, encircling the four receding areas of Dholavira, were not meant for defence but to control the movement of goods and to safeguard 'craft production'. We have walls around our factories and our Special Economic Zones for the same reason.

We stepped down past pillars which could have been gate-posts, into the enormous stadium. It stretched for 193 m by 49 m and had tiered seating all around. Of all the million square kilometres once covered by this mysterious civilisation, in our sub-continent, Dholavira is the only Harappan city with a stadium. Scholars believe that this unique place could accommodate 10,000 people with special seating for the VIPs who lived in the Citadel. The stadium was used for ceremonials, festivals and sports and one of the activities was bull-leaping where agile, naked, young women grabbed the horns of a bull and somersaulted over the enraged animal. It was an extreme sport popular in parts of the Mediterranean of that age.

Bulls have been depicted in many of the clay seals found in Dholavira, and displayed in the Museum. Bullocks had been used to draw water from a deep well on the broad East-West road to fill a storage tank at this level. "How did the well get its water?" we asked our guide. "No one is sure," he said. "It was either by seepage from the big reservoirs or, perhaps, there is an underground channel which has not been discovered as yet. But there is an underground channel linking this tank which supplied drinking water, to another tank used for bathing. That tank was drained by pulling out a plug, just like in ceramic tubs in five-star hotels!"

Hygiene was an obsession with the people of Dholavira, every house had a bathroom with its sewerage being drained into a cesspit. "That was more than 3,000 years before Europeans made something similar," remarked our guide, proudly. We were beginning to get the impression of a tightly controlled civic society, much like those in the old trading forts set up by the East India Company. In fact the Middle Town, at a level below the Bailey, was the residential area of the burghers, the solid middle-class traders who form the stabilising ballast of most societies. Here, the stone foundations showed houses of regimented similarity set in streets laid out in a disciplined grid pattern.

Here, too, had been found the greatest evidence of a strong central authority enforcing its writ. The sizes of bricks and dressed stones, the unerring accuracy of weights and measures, the design of edge-stones at the angles of walls, all these were exactly the same everywhere in Dholavira. In fact, though the people of this industrial city imported raw materials from far-flung sources, turned them into ornaments and stone blades, and exported them under their individual trademark seals, they steadfastly resisted being influenced by their foreign associates. It was almost as if their leaders had said, "Look, we have a good thing going. Why should we change?"

It was only in the Lower Town that the civic planners seemed to have allowed a relaxation from their rigid formality. This was the factory and labour-lines area. Here, we believe, was where the brick kilns and forges

The seals that pre-dated trademarks.

Outlines of later bhunga *huts.*

had stood, belching out smoke which the winds off the Rann had carried away from the elite areas of Dholavira. The kilns and the forges had had a voracious appetite for wood, and so the forests had been felled. With the loss of green cover, the bay had been silted up, rising levels of saline water had destroyed the fields. But long generations of conformity had robbed the Dholavirans of their ability to think out of the box. This was about the time, in 2,000 BC, that the great markets of Sumeria began to decline because of political upheavals. At first we had believed, along with many others, that Indo-Iranians from the steppes had delivered the final blow to this civilisation. The latest research does not support this view.

In the once-exclusive 'Citadel' we saw the stone walls of circular huts with a central base-stone to hold a pole supporting a thatched roof. Such '*bhunga*' huts are still common in rural areas of the Rann. When their support systems and export markets had withered away, the civilised but impoverished urbanites of Dholavira had abandoned their city and squatters had moved in.

We had still not discovered who these Dholavirans were. Excavations have uncovered only about one-tenth of the ancient city. Apart from the seals and the signboard no other records have been found and their language remains a mystery. Perhaps further diggings will unearth trading and civic records inscribed on clay, soapstone or even on copper. Some scholars claim that they spoke and wrote in an early version of Tamil, but that is still speculation. For more scientific conclusions we went to our most authoritative scientists: I.S. Bisht and Dr. P. Ajithprasad.

According to them, the Dholavirans were a seafaring people who could have sailed in when the Rann was an arm of the Arabian Sea. They were also urban immigrants who had set up their sophisticated city in what was, then, a rural area. Here, the Dholavirans had found a people 'who were unfamiliar with advanced technology of pottery making, use of copper and other attributes of the civilised world.' The Dholavirans had chosen this location because it was central to their sources of raw materials like shells, crystals, glass sand, coloured clays and minerals. The main overseas market was the advanced empire of Sumeria.

The world's first street sign: 'Entry of Two-Wheelers Prohibited'?

Beads such as these were exported to West Asia.

Earlier we had thought that the Harappans were Sumerian colonists, BC versions of the East India Company's expatriates. We now believe that they were Indians of Mediterranean stock, descendants of ancient Dravidian immigrants of the same race as the Sumerians. Because of their racial affinity, they found it as easy to establish commercial bonds with the Sumerians as the Brits and the Americans do today. But, as we have said, their stubborn refusal to adapt, to find new products, or new markets, led these pre-Aryan people to their downfall. Dholavira died. Dust and soil covered its ruins, shrubs spread.

And the little gerbils moved in again.

The Jackals Came After Aarti

THE BANNI LANDS

In the Banni lands we lived in a *bhunga*.

On an earlier trip we had learnt that the Banni were grasslands at the edge of the saline Rann. They had been made fertile by seasonal torrents spreading silt over them every monsoon. In the elegant Shaam-e-Sarhad Village Resort at Hodka, Kachch, we learnt all about *bhunga*s.

Circular, thatched, *bhunga*, huts rose at one end of a large, saucer-shaped compound floored with mud-plaster. Inside the huts there were a few luxuries for the sophisticated traveller: beds on earthen platforms with thick and very comfortable mattresses, cushioned seating against the walls. The complex mud-and-mirror work of Gujarat gave an understated elegance to our hut. The outer walls were painted with traditional abstract designs in coloured earths, standing out dramatically against the mud plaster. An information board in the resort said:

Hodka's Shaam-e-Sarhad Village Resort.

A Banni Pathan *rides his steed.*

> Our elders tell us that the *bhunga* was invented after the 1819 earthquake. The circular form works as an arch on the lateral movement of an Earthquake strongly holding the walls together. As the sun-baked earth bricks complete the plinths and rooms, the women in our families embellish the space with mud murals, coloured earth paintings and mirrors.

An interesting tradition but, after what we saw in the ruins of the Harappan city of Dholavira, it was likely that its earthquake-resistant design had been part of a protohistoric tradition.

That was just the beginning of our encounters with the Banni people's living links with their intriguing past.

The resort was patrolled by the hawk-nosed, eagle-eyed Pandhi Kheyali Haleputra. He said he was a *Banni Pathan*. He had the lean, Clint Eastwood, look of a man whose ancestors had sniped at intruding Brits in the rugged Khyber Pass! But, equally clearly, Pandhi was a Banni man. And so, after considerable persuasion, we convinced our guide, Salim, to take us to a Banni Pathan village after we promised not to reveal the name of the village.

"They are conservative and they don't want insensitive tourists to spoil the attitudes of their community."

The village was a long and rugged ride away and we lost our way twice in that featureless terrain. We thought of the legend of Mekran Dada of the Banni Lands. He could have been an 18th century Sufi saint sanctified in folk memory. Today, with his spectral donkey Laliya and dog Motiya, his spirit rescues travellers who are sick or have lost their way in this trackless plain. Happily, we did not have to call upon him because we had come to a rough fence of logs and thorn-scrub identifying the Banni Pathan village.

Our throats were raspy with dust and our muscles and joints had taken a beating. But perhaps our travel-worn appearance helped: we didn't resemble the short-shorts-and-singlet types that were unwelcome here. In fact our wary hosts seemed to thaw only when they learnt that we were from the Himalayas. Memories of their mountainous homeland had probably struck the right chord.

The women brought out their embroidery, cups of tea were drunk and the ice was broken.

Three hundred years ago, they said, they had been brought here by their leader. "This was a very rich grassland then," they said, "But now, in many places the desert is moving in." The people were tall and wiry with aquiline noses and amber eyes. The men wore kurta-pyjamas, or kurtas and lungis. A few wore shirts and trousers. The women were more traditionally attired with headscarves and the long-skirted embroidered dresses of this region. As in most communities, wedding traditions are the last to change. A man put on a groom's mask of bright beads interspersed with fragrant cloves. It

Above: Close-up of a Banni Pathan's *nuptial mask.*

Left: A bridegoom's mask.

The men led us to the stables where they keep their beautiful Kathiawari and Sindhi horses. "We have maintained our Afghan tradition of being horse breeders," said Abdullah with considerable pride. He mounted his horse, Vijiri, and galloped bareback around a dusty field, sending goats skittering in fright.

covered him from his forehead to his chest and must have taken weeks of painstaking work. It's called a *Moad*. He also carried a *Kothri*, bead purse in which grooms carried peppermint, cloves and other sweet-smelling spices which they would distribute to their friends. We couldn't persuade a woman to wear the *Akhiyo* bride's mask, but a man agreed. It covered his face and resembled a crocheted mat with two large eyeholes

In this seemingly inhospitable land of grass and thorn, a migrant community had made a home and preserved their customs and traditions for over three centuries. Obviously, it was not as unwelcoming a land as we had imagined. Or perhaps the austerity of the land, the lack of civic amenities, breeds a tough self reliance, encourages creativity because of the absence of other diversions.

In the slightly grimy village of Nirona we discovered the radiant art of *rogan*. *Rogan* designs are created on fabrics using an intricate technique involving castor-oil boiled-down to the consistency of a tacky resin. Holding reed pens, *rogan* artists draw pictures as intricately delicate as fine embroidery. It once used to embellish costumes but cheaper, factory produced, prints virtually wiped it out. Then a far-seeing member of a Muslim Khatri family decided to raise it from a utility craft into an art form. Khatri Sumar Daud, who had won a National award for his work in 2003, assured us that only his family has preserved, and developed, this rare art.

Right: A craftsman tests the consistency of the rogan *'resin'.*
Facing page: The wetlands of the Rann.

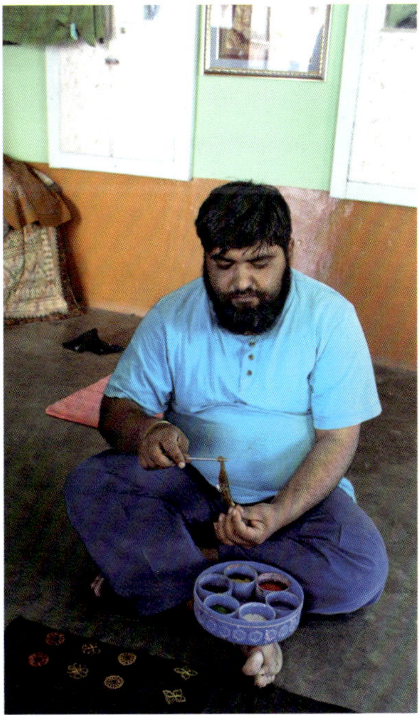

After the discovery of *rogan* we unearthed a treasure trove of cottage skills among the Banni people, including an unusual water-harvesting one. Just outside a village, we clambered over a wooden stile and into a large, gentle, depression shaded by spreading trees. Not far from the stile was a cemented trough filled with water. And all around were wells, some of which had been abandoned and partially filled with earth. One of the wells was still in use and had water about nine metres down. This was a working *Virda*: a seepage well. We looked in, fascinated. It was lined with fairly close fitting logs up to two metres from the top, the spaces between the logs being stuffed with ferns to allow water to trickle in. From there on the walls of the well were made of tightly packed ferns wadded together. A villager who had ambled up explained that *Virda*s were always built in low-lying ground, preferably where there were mango trees because they indicated the presence of water-saturated soil.

"No one can say how long a *Virda* will last: maybe many years, maybe a few weeks. We fill up the old ones that dry up, make new ones."

"Can anyone draw water from a *Virda*?"

"That is not our custom. Water is very precious, it must not be spoilt. So we choose from volunteers. They draw water from the *Virda*s and fill the trough for the village."

"How long has this *Virda* been giving you water?"

He smiled and nodded. "This is a very good *Virda*. Many times we have renewed the logs and the filtering ferns. It has served us for 300 years and its water is sweeter than your packaged drinking water."

He looked around, shouted, and loped away, scaring cattle that were trying to climb over the stile.

We wondered how many generations of trial and error it had taken to develop the *Virda* techniques. As we said, the Banni's trove of rural skills is enormous. We visited cottages where they did embroidery and appliqué, wood carving and pottery and lac-ware and created stuffed toys of dancers and camels and turbaned riders on horses. Luhar Salemamad Husen forged

Bellmaker Salim Moha at work: cattle bells to chimes.

bells. His craft grew out of fashioning bells for herders so that they could identify their foraging animals. He showed us wind-bells and festoons of love-bells shaped like hearts and even a mini xylophone called a *sa-re-ga-ma*, the do-re-me-fa of Indian music. He creates his bells of iron, hammers them till they produce the right sound, then plates them in copper. "I can produce any tone you want," he asserted confidently.

The sounds of the Banni Lands were a gentle orchestration as we drove through the scrub wilderness: the *clonk-tonk* of buffalo bells from the half-wild black herds; the twitter-whistle of partridges insistent in the sere grass; the honking of an enormous squadron of cranes winging in the soft light of evening; the distant, lonely, yowl of a jackal setting off a cacophonous chorus of howls like demented spirits beckoning from

A housewife creates an appliqued garment.

Jackals feasting on temple offerings.

the underworld. "They are singing for their supper," remarked a gaunt man with deep-set eyes in the parking lot of the Dattatreya temple. The shrine is perched atop a knoll in the Black Hills of Kachch, wreathed in an eerie legend.

A board at the temple said:

> Welcome to the top of the Black Hills! From this 1,437 ft peak you can see the Great Rann of Kachchh, the salt desert, spread over long distances in all three directions. Millions of years ago these hills and the land were under the sea. Look carefully and you may find the evidence—fossilised shells on these rocks. The temple priests here practice an age-old tradition of offering food to the jackals. The common folklore is that when there was no food to offer to these jackals, the Pir of Pachchmai, also known as Dattatreya, the Hindu deity, offered a part of his body. To this day, at sunset, the jackals come every day to receive their food at the hands of the priest.

The man with the deep-set eyes, seeing us reading the legend, added, "Dattatreya is said to have called out 'Lo ang' which is 'Take my body'. The priests still echo that self sacrificing call, even now. Come, the *aarti* is over. It is almost time."

We thanked him, hurried, and joined a mass of devotees, assembled on a spur, gazing down at a platform built at the edge of the thorny cactus

Sunset over the salt lands.

thickets. A priest approached, carrying a large bowl of consecrated food. He struck the bowl, emptied its contents on the platform, called out. And suddenly, the cactus thickets shifted and moved as a horde of dun-coloured jackals materialised out of the khaki shadows of the scrub, leapt on the platform and, snarling and yapping, began to feast on the *prasad*. It was an amazing sight and one that had been repeated every day ever since this sacred hillock emerged out of the salt-flats of the Rann, thrust up by the earthquake of 1918. Or so a priest of the temple informed us very solemnly. "This was," he added, "on the caravan route from our land to the other side of the Rann, now in Pakistan."

We couldn't quite establish the contours of the route in our minds but then, possibly, our topographical knowledge wasn't quite up to his.

We walked to the parapet at the far edge of the escarpment that fell away from the shrine. At our feet, the vast expanse of the saline flats beyond the scrub wilderness shimmered like crushed glass, stretching to the curve of the earth's shoulder. The sun was an angry ball at the edge of the world, sinking slowly, implacably. For a brief moment the salt flats picked up its reflection and then, after a swift and almost imperceptible, flash of green, the sun was swallowed by the dusk. The sky stretched velvet black over it all, spangled with increasing mirror-chips of stars.

And as we drove down from the knoll, a cool night wind, scented of incense, brought the far yowl of a jackal choir-master. Then, on cue, a full-throated chorale burst out, celebrating the drama of sunset on the far frontiers of the Banni Lands.

Land of the Nomads

THE LITTLE RANN

The peacock had woken us with a piercing and adenoidal *ciaow*!

His name was Tom and he was one of the many unusual service-providers in the Rann Riders Resort in Saurashtra's Dasada. And so, the stars were still sequinning the sky when we drove out, through the chill pre-dawn, heading for the Little Rann.

This 4,000 sq km featureless plain is a nomadic land. Every year its contours change subtly. It boundaries move inland in one season and then back towards the shore in the next. It gets submerged when monsoon storms push in the waters of the Arabian Sea. Then when the sea retreats it leaves shape-shifting strands of glittering salt crystals on the cement-hard surface, and sloshes around underneath. In some places, large purple ocular patches of saline water appear in the shimmering expanse of white like a big bruised eye. It's an alien, inhospitable, land at first glance. But we had been told that it held a rich diversity of life.

And, right on cue, life appeared.

Flamingoes in the wetlands of the Rann.

A desert fox is intrigued by us.

On a reedy channel, just before we reached the Rann, a brace of Whistling Teals ducked their heads under the surface, emerged, swallowed, and then quacked in contentment. Closer to us an Open-billed Stork stood gazing morosely into the water. Stillness was his strategy, encouraging inquisitive fish to venture within impaling reach of his beak. And, as we watched, two other storks circled in and landed in a chevron of ripples. Unlike their contemplative cousin, they began wading and spear-fishing immediately. Clearly, this marshy stretch offered a rich broth of goodies for these water birds.

The rising sun was a red eggshell peeping over the horizon when we left the channel and bumped over the cracked surface of the Rann. Nothing moved except a chill wind stirring the scattered thorn thickets. These tough, salt-tolerant, plants can stand up to most of the battering of the Rann and their bristly clumps break the monotony of the grey expanse of wrinkled clay of the Rann. Just when we were beginning to tire of the endless uniformity of the terrain, our driver snapped, "Desert Fox!" and pointed. We frowned, scanned, searched. Nothing. Clipped on our zooms. Panned. There! He was dun coloured, merging with the dull landscape. The fox puppy had large ears…their acute hearing plays a major role in their survival…large eyes and was quite fearless. He was sitting up when we spotted him. Then he settled down on his tummy. Finally, bored with all the clicking and moving, he stood up, turned and vanished into his den at the base of the thicket.

He must have been the most adventurous of his siblings because foxes, like dogs, produce litters of 4 to 6 pups. If we had trudged across and peered in, we'd probably have seen his siblings skulking in the den. Since the parents were nowhere in sight, they must have been out hunting. Foxes generally bond for life and hunt together, running for many kilometres at speeds of over 30 kms per hour. In the inhospitable wilderness of the Rann, they would have to cover a wide area to bring back food for their cubs. But they aren't choosy about their diet and, in coastal areas such as these, they prey on water-birds' chicks and eggs, snap up crabs and fish stranded in drying pools.

Here, foxes were the largest land predators and had nothing to fear.

Our jeep had just started again when we spotted two large, slowly moving, shadows. As we drove up to them they froze. This is a favoured Nilgai tactic: emulate a statue and hope you'll be mistaken for a boulder! Then the lighter-coloured cow moved. It began to nibble the young leaves of the thorn bushes, bent its head and munched on the stubby grass that thrust up through the cracks in the surface of the Rann.

We had always associated Bluebells with open grasslands and cultivation and so we were surprised to find them in this coastal area. But they seemed to have become well-adjusted to these saline flood-plains thriving in the absence of their main enemy, the irate farmer! They were quite fearless, looking at us with a certain chin-raised arrogance, nostrils flaring speculatively.

Now, suddenly, this uninviting salt desert began to teem with wildlife. A herd of beautiful, fawn-and-white, wild asses appeared as if out of a shimmering desert mirage and ambled past. But when our jeep moved to get closer, they began to trot, and then they galloped. Slightly larger than donkeys they are fiercely independent animals who have never been tamed. The fluidity of their motion was superb. Once, many years ago, we had been driven by a Forest Officer who had been asked to clock the speed of these swift animals. He had given chase to a herd and even when his speedometer was hovering beyond the 60 kmph mark, the last animals in the herd ahead were splattering clay on our windscreens with their fleeing hooves! The Forest Department has done a good job in protecting these endangered animals. In 1946 there were between 3,000 to 5,000 of them

The herd of wild asses galloped away, swiftly.

but epidemics had devastated their numbers. Today, however, thanks to strict conservation, their population is increasing. These *Ghudkhar*s are so attuned to their environment that they can sense when the Rann is likely to be flooded. They congregate on the little hillocks, called *Bet*s, which dot the saline plains, and stay there till the waters recede.

Not all inhabitants of the Rann resent the presence of sea water. A pump thudded like an erratic heart spouting sub-surface brine into flat, shallow, pans. There the scorching heat of the sun sucked up the water and left white encrustations of salt. This was raked up by salt-pan workers, packed into bags, and trucked out to chemical factories and table-salt manufacturers.

Heading back to the cool of the Rann Riders Resort, we stopped at an encampment of *Maldhari* herdsmen. The word *maldhari* is a generic term for all herdsmen. These nomads were, more specifically, *Wagodia Rabari*s. They are nomads, driving their flocks of sheep and goats from one pastureland to the next. The women lead their laden camels, dogs guard both the caravans and the flocks, and though the moustached and turbaned men are, traditionally, dressed in white, their ladies wear a resplendence of jewellery and brightly embroidered blouses and skirts. They also tattoo their hands and necks with tiny motifs which are believed to be auspicious symbols to ward off evil. We asked them where they were going. "Not far," said a pretty young woman, leading a galumphing camel, "We will make camp a little before sunset."

Above: Women gossip before leaving with their camel caravans.
Facing page: Workers raking in salt from a pan.

For us the heat, reflecting off the clayey surface of the Rann, had become oppressive. We returned to the cool comfort of our resort and, when we sat down to breakfast on the tree-shaded lawns, we were joined by our plumed alarm clock, Tom the peacock. Tom, we learnt, is rather finicky about his food and particular about the way it's served. It has to be dry cornflakes, always in a bowl, preferably on a dining table.

His close companions are Dick, a mongoose who lives in an earthen pot when he's not out scouring the grounds for noxious creatures; and Harry, the cat who has his own space in the kitchen. They form the core team of the Vermin Guard of the resort. They are assisted by the jet black contingent of the *Khadaknath* fowls: black feathers, black combs, black flesh. These are the alert pest controllers, snapping up insects and other creepy crawlies with gusto. They came from Jhabua in Madhya Pradesh where they are, apparently, used in black magic: condemned because of their colour!

We recalled that one of the *Maldhari* camels had carried a bamboo crate with cocks and hens. But all those birds were brown and red, not black. We forgot to ask if they were a regular part of the caravan or temporary members being carried for a celebratory feast when the women set up camp.

This must have happened before we drove out that evening. We passed an encampment of camel-breeders with a herd of dromedaries and their calves like cuddly stuffed toys. The breeders attribute their vigorous good health and longevity to a steady diet of camel milk. One of us drank it regularly at breakfast in a very upscale hotel in Dubai. It had the taste and consistency of reconstituted milk meant for babies and was very sustaining. It went particularly well with fresh dates and we thought of it when we drove past a long line of date palms after leaving the resort on our evening jeep safari.

A little before sunset we drew up on the banks of the *Nawa Talab*, a shimmering spread of briny water dotted with marshy islands. A Spoonbill stood, meditatively, in a green reed bed. We stepped out of our jeep. Tacky clay squelched under our feet and a cacophony of squawking, rasping, croaking, splashing sounds grew. This estuarine lake was alive with flocks of long-legged Cranes, bag-beaked Pelicans and high-stepping Flamingos with their curved, food filtering bills, stalking solemnly. All three are migrants, nomads of the bird world. Most of the Flamingos were daubed with pink thanks to a rich diet of shrimp. We squelched closer. The birds stopped feeding, raised their graceful heads slowly. We raised our cameras. The lake erupted in a silver spray as the birds took off, quacking, grunting, honking; soared; filled the sky with a flickering, feathery, canopy as if a legion of angels was wheeling overhead. We stood for a long while, gazing up at them in awe. And then we trod back to our jeep.

Clearly, the seemingly inhospitable saline desert of the Little Rann was alive and burgeoning.

The Pugmarks of History

SASAN GIR

We went in search of the most honoured animals in the world.

Three heraldic lions had stood tall in the Royal Coat of Arms over every country of the erstwhile British Empire. Long before that, Richard the Lion Heart had fought under them in his West Asian Crusade in the 12th century. At that time, Asian lions had roamed across many of those lands, from Northern Turkey through Arabia to Northern India up to the Narmada. The Emperor Ashoka chose four lions as the capital of his pillars. This became the National Emblem of India. People began to name themselves after this magnificent big cat: Sher, Singh, Sinh, Sinha, Narasimha. But as humans increased, the animals decreased. By the end of the 19th century there were an estimated 12 left in the whole world, all of them in a small thorn forest in the former princely state of Junagadh. Alarmed, the Nawab banned the hunting of lions. Today, the only place in the world where such magnificent animals live free is in the protected wilderness in Gujarat's Gir. Their population has grown to 114.

A fat partridge eyes visitors, fearlessly.

The grounds of Sinh Sadan.

This, in turn, has strengthened the web-of-life, the entire ecology, of Gir.

This year, when spring was warming into summer, we drove into the green campus of the Gujarat Forest Department's Sinh Sadan. Many visitors had flocked into the hamlet of Sasan Gir, and so we had to take the second round that morning, missing our favoured dawn tour. Lions prefer hunting at night, settling down to sleep when the sun begins to rise. But even though we didn't expect to sight a lion on that forenoon safari, we drove around anyway. We're glad we did: we had the jungle to ourselves.

Gir National Park spreads over 258.7 sq kms as a National Park, 1,153.4 sq kms as a Sanctuary and 470.5 sq kms as a Buffer Zone. This gently undulating terrain is covered with very dry teak forests, dry deciduous scrub forests and grasslands. Seven rivers flow through Gir but they seem to be rather fickle, depending on the rains, except for the perennial Hiran. A railway line passes through part of the sanctuary and, in one of our rounds, we had to wait for a slow train to chug past. So much for the topography.

For us, it was just the right season for wildlife spotting. Most trees had shed their leaves and forest workers were sweeping them up to prevent forest fires. Consequently, visibility was clear for fairly long distances. When an animal at the top of the food chain is protected then everything lower down is also nurtured. There were herds of chital, their speckled coats flickering through the sun-dappled forest. Clans of langurs had teamed up with the spotted deer, dropping leaves and fruit to the chital grazing on the forest floor. From their high view-point atop trees, they would also spot predators approaching from far away. Their hooting warning would alert the deer to flee, flashing the white on their tails as danger signals to other animals. This late in the morning, however, most of the predators were asleep and even peacocks, with their beautiful, and ungainly, tails pecked at their breakfast with the deliberate fastidiousness of gourmets.

This is the best time to do bird-watching and though most of Gir's forests had the usual assortment of doves, wood-peckers, questing parrots and garrulous babblers, we did see a Spotted Owlet, fluffed up like a sage in a downy coat, a brace of fat partridges who seemed as curious about us as we were about them, and a brilliantly painted kingfisher. He glittered in a spring-green valley, perched on a branch above a chortling jungle stream. If it hadn't been for the lions, the trees would probably have been cut for firewood, the stream would have dried and the birds would have found their way to greener pastures.

Not all birds prefer the shade of spreading, green, trees. Some have adapted to a more austere environment. This bird was so perfectly camouflaged on the open forest strewn with sere leaves, that we missed it. And even after our driver had stopped the jeep and the guide had pointed it out, we would not have seen it if it had not moved. Then we spotted it. The Stone Curlew was sitting on her eggs in a shallow nest scooped out of the leaves and pebbles, her male keeping guard nearby. They are also known as 'thick knees' because of their arthritic-looking joints but they didn't seem to object to us though, on our return, the hen had taken a break and was foraging but within sight of her two, mottled, eggs.

Much further on, we spotted a female jackal chewing on a hunk of meat. It, too, was quite unperturbed by our presence, continuing with its meal as if it had all the time in the world. Such fearless behaviour generally indicates a well-protected environment, free of poachers as well as other human disturbance.

But we still hadn't seen any lions though, when we returned to Sinh Sadan, a family from Mumbai was as bubbly as champagne. All of them had seen and photographed a whole pride of lions: a full-maned lion, two lionesses, and three

A Black Ibis perched on a tree in Sinh Sadan.

Left: This jackal went on to enjoy its kill unperturbed by our presence. Below: Chital, alert at the sound of danger.

cubs. "I wanted to get out of the jeep and cuddle them" gushed 10-year old Sania, "but their mother might have bitten me. No?" We agreed that that might have happened but that didn't dampen her enthusiasm one little bit!

A heron waits in a stream in the lion's protected habitat.

A blackbuck in the Gir Interpretation Zone, Safari Park.

Sania had some advice for us. "Uncle-Auntyji, if you want to see lions, definitely go to the Safari Park. Some lions, if they are sick, are in cages, so doctors can treat them. No? But some lions roam around and even hunt. My *mamaji*, when he came here, two-three years ago, saw a lion in the Safari Park killing a blackbuck. That's sad for the blackbuck, no? But the lion has to eat too. Right?"

Her mother intervened. "That's enough, Sonu. She's a great talker!"

"But I haven't finished yet. So maybe if you go to the Safari Park you'll see a lion hunting. Though they say that only the lionesses hunt and the lion sits back like a big dada and then he has the right to scoff while the others sit back. Very macho, No?"

We were impressed by her knowledge and were quite prepared to listen to more but her mother smiled, nodded, and hurried her away. We decided to follow Sania's advice. We took a trip into the Safari Park, carrying a snack we picked up on the way.

The Safari Park, formally called The Gir Interpretation Zone is at Devalia, 12 kms from Sinh Sadan. It covers 412 hectares of the same terrain as the drier parts of the Gir National Park: thorn scrub and grasslands. All entrances have animal-excluding double gates. The first gate is opened. A car enters. The gate is closed. Only then is the gate in front opened to allow the vehicle to drive into the Park.

Most of the animals, the lions and their prey species, are allowed to roam freely around the zone, but there are a few infirmary cages with fenced-in

A brilliant kingfisher watches over a pool in a watered valley.

enclosures for sick animals to walk around when they are recouping. We saw a rather lazy old lion snoozing in his cage, and a far more active lioness pacing her enclosure gazing at two blackbucks, on the other side of her fence, speculatively. But we didn't see any lions outside the cages.

The well-informed Dr. Sandeep Kumar, IFS, Deputy Conservator of Forests and boss of Gir, assured us that we would probably have better luck in the afternoon round of Gir. He put us in the hands of guide Ketan, who was also a photographer, and driver Ashish. We were told that they were very lucky: in animal spotting luck plays a major role. And it seemed to change immediately.

We passed a *Maldhari* grazing his buffaloes just outside a rather make-shift village. In Gir, these semi-nomadic herdsmen are divided into a number of tribes like *Bharwads*, *Charan*s, *Ahir*s and *Kathi*s. They have lived here for so long, in their settlements called *nesses*, that they have become part of the ecosystem. The lions of Gir seem to accept them as fellow forest dwellers and, unlike African Lions, they do not attack these people. They do, however, prey on their cattle but the official guide-book on Gir said:

> About 25 per cent of the lion's food comes from the livestock of the *Maldhari*s. Yet the wise old men of the community, in spite of being poor, do not accept monetary compensation from the government when their

> cattle are killed by the lions. They believe it is like offering a token fee for staying in the lions' home. Will the same value system continue with the generation next?

Possibly not, as pressure on the land increases and the lion population grows in numbers.

The young man we spoke to had abandoned the traditional white turban and robes of his ancestors for shirt and trousers. He said a lion had been seen not far from his settlement this morning and his herd of buffaloes was still restless. If a lion had been spotted in the morning the chances were that it had not wandered too far after dawn. That encouraged us.

We drove on and passed a water tanker filling a trough built by the Forest Department. The tanker was manned by an interesting community of Gir: the *Siddhis*. We spoke to some of them later, and learnt that they believed that their ancestors had come from Uganda. They looked of African origin and claimed that they had been brought here by the Nawab of Junagadh as agriculturists. They speak Gujarati, are Sunni Muslims, and try to maintain their bloodlines though, as a young man remarked, "If someone falls in love with an outsider, what can we do? If they return to our community all we insist on is that they get married according to our rites. Nowadays we work as labourers and are helping the Forest Department preserve the National Park."

We waited for a while, allowing the water tanker to move on. Less than fifteen minutes later, a herd of chital arrived, and started drinking at the trough.

The Siddhis of Gir claimed that their ancestors came from Uganda.

At last, we spotted a lioness.

We drove on, passed a Nilgai bull standing stock-still against a huge, overshadowing, banyan tree. It wasn't grazing but was as immobile as a blue-grey boulder. We wondered, for a moment, if it had seen a big cat, but then it moved and began to nibble at some leaves. A little later we heard a strange sound and our companions claimed that it was the alarm call of a Sambar. They said its nervousness could have been triggered by our presence. It needn't, necessarily, have sensed a predator approaching.

The sun was quite low in the sky, the light had softened, and we were giving up hope of ever spotting one of the lions of Gir when we heard the *yap*! of a frightened Spotted Deer. Three of them were just off the road, a little ahead of us. We drove up and saw that they were standing rigid, their ears swivelled forward. Danger lay in front of them and they were ready to scoot.

We raced ahead. Ketan mentioned a wooded ravine as a likely spot. We drove into it. Stopped. Then we sat riveted to our seats as we gazed at the rare and heraldic animal that had drawn us to this very special place. There, in the half-shadows of the forest floor, stretched out in regal ease, was a magnificent lioness. She turned her head and looked at us with serene arrogance, the sunlight glowing on her amber eyes.

Then, when we had taken all the pictures we wanted, she rose and, very languidly, vanished into the protected forests of Gir.

Hamlet of the Holy Fire

UDWADA

In Gujarat, we visited the last settlement of the Aryans.

Iconic scholar, Lokmanya Bal Gangadhar Tilak, had shown us the way. In his book *The Arctic Home in the Vedas* he had said that the 'Indo-Aryans' had been compelled to leave their original home and migrate, 'the Indians to the east and the Persians to the west.' That little nugget remained lodged in our memories like a seed waiting to sprout. Years later a Parsi friend had asked us the origin of the term 'Anglo-Indian'. We had referred him to Article 366 of the Constitution, and then we'd asked,

"Why are you called 'Parsis'?"

"Because when we fled persecution and landed in India, in 697, people asked us where we had come from and we said 'Pars' or 'Fars'. That was the old name for Persia or Iran. So they called us 'Parsis'"

"Had Parsis been persecuted in Iran?"

"We weren't called Parsis, then. We were Zoroastrians, as we still are: followers of the Prophet Zarathushtra. When the great Sassanian Empire fell, in Persia, under the onslaught of a fanatical conqueror, he wanted us to convert to his faith and began to destroy our temples and our way of

A panel depicts Ahura Mazda and Zoroaster.

life. So we fled. We had been told that Hindus were very tolerant of other faiths, so we chose India. Eventually, under the leadership of our priest, Dastur Nairyoshang Dhawal, the first batch of our people sailed away and landed in Diu."

"And were you welcomed?"

He laughed. "Oh yes. But Diu was a port and we were neither sailors nor fishermen. We were agriculturists. So we moved to Sanjan. There, according to a legend, Jadi Rana, the king, sent us a bowl full of milk to indicate that his kingdom was brimming over with people and so he could not accept any more. But our elders were wise. They put a spoonful of sugar in the milk. The milk did not spill over. They said, 'In this way will we merge with your people and sweeten your society without disturbing it.' But if you're really interested in getting the full story, go to Udwada."

We made notes of that conversation and, eventually, we did visit this spiritual capital of the Zoroastrians.

It was disappointing at first. There was nothing monumental or spectacularly historic about it. There was no Taj Mahal of the Mughals or soaring Brihadeshwarar of the Cholas. We didn't see anything like the assertion of the might of Empire like Delhi's North and South Block or even impressive alien icons like the Chinese Fishing Nets of Fort Cochin. Udwada is a serene, old, laid-back, town. As we drove slowly down the main

Above: A typical quiet street in Udwada.
Facing page: A model of a Parsi priest attending to the Sacred Fire.

A serene resident looks out from her verandah.

street, that first evening, senior citizens in black skull caps chatted gently on swings in their verandahs, gracefully aging old mansions with wrought-iron balconies rose on either side, and there was a sense of undisturbed, middle-class, gentility as if the winds of the hurrying world had been subdued to a soft whisper here. Udwada calls itself a town but, today, it is gently mellowing down into a hamlet. We didn't realise, at the time, that this was really the essence of the Parsi ethos: an inbred urbanity that shuns ostentation. At the heart of it, however, and binding the entire diaspora of the Parsis, is a great temple where a sacred fire has been burning for one thousand three hundred years. Statues of the winged lions, with human faces and beards, stood at the foot of the flight of steps leading up to the door of the temple. We saw this from the gate but a watchman said that only Parsis could go in. We could not understand why the hospitable Parsis forbade people of

A couple from Mumbai drives to Udwada every month.

A beautiful wrought iron railing glitters on an old mansion.

other faiths from entering their temple. It seemed to go against their well-deserved reputation for warm-hearted hospitality. We decided to learn more about these intriguing people.

When we told our hostess, Zenobia, owner of the heritage Globe Hotel, about our quest, she said, "The Zoroastrian Information Centre is not far away. You should visit it."

The next morning, we did. It was excellent. We had budgeted half an hour for the visit, we stayed more than two and even then we had not seen

Verandah swings are a common feature in Udwada.

The towering gateway to the Fire Temple.

everything. It was a mind-blowing experience. We thought of our many Parsi friends and wondered why they had not made more of their remarkable heritage. Here, in the rooms of this restored old mansion, we saw a smitten people leaving everything behind them and fleeing to a distant land, an alien land, just because they wanted to preserve their faith. We saw these refugees pulling themselves up by their bootstraps, in India, helping others even as they helped themselves. We thought back: we had never seen a Parsi beggar, never met anyone of that small community who had been a burden on Indian society. They had never asked for handouts, or reservations even though they were a tiny minority, never agitated to arm-twist the government to accede to their demands: they did not make demands. For that matter, there was a curious absence of Parsi politicians, which, in itself, seemed significant. And yet, while looking after themselves, they had shared their wealth with all citizens, set up cultural institutions and industries noted for the way they looked after their employees. Their honour roll displayed in the Centre, was stupendous: world famous industrialists, lawyers, doctors, scientists, philanthropists, a towering Chief Justice of India. They didn't need American millionaires to advise them to give to charity, they've been doing it on their own for more than a century.

And they had managed to do all this with a significant absence of trumpet-blowing.

That, perhaps, was their greatest fault: they were still reluctant to tom-tom their myriad achievements.

In this Information Centre, tucked away in an insignificant part of a small, self-effacing hamlet, we also learnt how these expatriates had survived by merging like sugar dissolving in milk while adhering to the customs and traditions of their ancient faith. We also learnt why non-Parsis are not allowed to enter their Temple.

According to an information board in the Centre, when the Parsis had wanted to settle in Sanjan, the king had asked them to accept certain pre-conditions:

- Their High Priest would explain the religion and its practices to the king.
- The men would lay down their arms and never take them up again.
- The migrants would abandon their own language and use the local language.
- The women would adopt the local dress.
- All ceremonies would be conducted after sunset.
- The Zoroastrians would not convert any of the king's subjects to their faith.
- Only the Zoroastrian people would be allowed to enter the Fire Temple.

To this day, the Parsis have lived up to all those promises made by their ancestors to a petty ruler of a small part of Gujarat, more than a thousand years ago. The only slight variation from those seven promises is the one about taking up arms. Parsis have headed the three Armed Forces of India and that list of chiefs includes the redoubtable Field Marshal Manekshaw. But no Parsi has ever taken up arms against the Indian state, so the spirit of the ancient promise remains untarnished.

Fire is revered by the Parsis as a manifestation of pure energy and though non-Parsis are not allowed to enter the Temple, there is a life-size model of the sanctum where the fire is enshrined, and of its attendant priest. This fire, called the Iranshah, was consecrated in India in 721 and has the fires taken from fifteen domestic and artisans' hearths, ovens and furnaces with the addition of fire ignited by lightning. Strangely, though the Parsis do not cremate their dead, fire from a funeral pyre has also been merged in the great Iranshah.

We filed away this odd fact and hoped that it would lead us on another significant trail later.

We drove out to Sanjan. Here, after all the holy materials and utensils had been brought from Iran, the Iranshah was consecrated in 721. Even the name of the fire enshrines the origins of the community. It was named the 'King of Iran' because the community had lost both their King and their country. In Sanjan we saw a tall, commemorative, pillar crowned by a sculpted flame, marking the consecration. Near it a Time Capsule has been buried so that future generations might discover the customs and traditions of their ancestors.

A memorial pillar to the creation of the holy Fire of the Parsis in Sanjan.

When we returned home, and were researching this chapter, the odd matter of fire from a funeral pyre being merged with the Iranshah surfaced in our minds again. Why did a community that does not cremate its dead include a crematorium fire in its most revered icon? We phoned Dasturji Khurshed Dastoor Kaikobad Dastoor, the Head Priest of the Iranshah, Udwada. We asked him if the inclusion of a cremation fire in the Iranshah could be the Zoroastrian's acknowledgement of the customs that existed in Iran before the birth of their prophet. He said, "It could be, it could be. But it could be because we should merge a fire taken from a human body, to include both the living and the dead."

Possibly. But according to the *Encyclopaedia Britannica*, in Vedic India, *asura* came to signify a kind of demon, *daiva* meant heavenly. In Iran, the terms were reversed: the *asura*s were extolled, to the exclusion of the *daiva*s, who were reduced to the rank of demons. Perhaps the Vedic herdsmen were forced out of Iran by the pre-Zoroastrian agriculturists: the historic Cain-Abel nomad-settler conflict. That could have been the reason why the gods of one became the demons of their rivals.

The two qualities that the Parsis are noted for are their integrity and empathy. They not only keep their word...as Ratan Tata said when he launched the Nano: 'A Promise is a Promise'...but their faith also encourages them to look at the world from another's point of view. These two qualities make for great leaders.

It is quite likely, then, that the empathic Parsis tried to build bridges with their old enemies, the Vedic people, by including the fire of their rivals' crematorium, when consecrating their revered Iranshah in Udwada...

Our Wondrous Water Pavilions

THE VAVS

They call them Step Wells; but that's a terribly, unimaginative, understatement. They have as much resemblance to wells as bullock-carts have to BMWs. Clearly for the 9th century Solanki dynasty, necessity was the mother of superb creativity. When the thirsty villages of Gujarat wanted water, their kings and queens gave them beautifully sculpted *vavs* that reached down to the water table. There, their people could rest in cool comfort, escaping the furnace heat of the summer sun. And while they rested, they could admire the sculptures and relive the great tales told by their epics and the brilliant array of folk beliefs that is the heritage of our land.

We visited one which, according to the Archaeological Survey of India, 'must have been the largest and most sumptuous structure of its kind.'

The Rani ki Vav is set in gently undulating grounds, shaded by occasional trees under which the ASI has placed a few benches. The entire, green, area is very popular. Students sat poring over their books, families picnicked, couples drifted around lost in their own world, and large groups of visitors headed for the sunken, and superbly carved, pavilions descending, tier after decorated tier, down to the water level far below.

The landscaped grounds of the Rani ki Vav.

We walked down a long flight of steps to the topmost of the many successive pavilions. From here on the *vav* was roofed and it was very cool and refreshingly damp after the dry heat of the surface. All around us, beautiful, and rather voluptuous, sculptures enriched the walls, pillars, lintels and virtually every available surface, except the ones we walked on.

At first glance, the principal theme appeared to be the ten incarnations of the Preserver of the Hindu Trinity: Lord Vishnu. In the words of the ASI, 'The figures include, the Lord of preservation, Vishnu, shown asleep on the coils of the multi-headed serpent, Ananta, which finds prominent position in the central niche on the different levels of the well.' We believe that ancient Indian thinkers had pre-empted Charles Darwin and gone beyond, well into the social evolution of *Homo sapiens*, ending with Bionic Man represented as the avatar to come, Kalki riding on a horse. But that is our personal view.

On a closer inspection, however, we realised that quite apart from the prevalence of vaishnavite figures, virtually all the diverse cult-figures of Hinduism had been depicted here. There were the ancient Mother Goddesses in many of their varied manifestations; we saw suggestions of the primeval snake deities probably dating back to pre-Vedic times, and some really evocative ones of beautiful celestial maidens putting on their make-up and their jewellery with all the seductiveness of a 21st century model. We recalled a fascinating thesis written by Dr. Malati J. Shendge, *The Civilised Demons: The Harappans in Rgveda*. She says that 'The human identity of the *Asuras*, the *Gandharvas*, the *Yaksas*, the *Pisacas*, the *Dasas*, the *Dasyus*, and the *Panis* is established.' Due to the all-embracing, eclectic, nature of Hinduism, these former opponents of the Vedic people were absorbed into their celestial pantheon. We were able to identify some of these beings in the graphic sculptures displayed in the intriguing *vav*. But since the ASI has put up barriers to prevent visitors from stepping into the western section of the *vav*, only half the estimated 800 sculptures can be seen by visitors. The east-west walkways are narrow and unfenced and so they could be dangerous for anyone who suffers from vertigo.

Interestingly, at the entrance there are a number of intricate designs that seem to represent the embroidered and woven patterns used in the handmade fabrics of Gujarat to this day. Though the *vav* was probably constructed by Udayamati, the queen of an 11th century Solanki ruler, in 1063, the concepts and forms depicted in this beautiful step well have a strangely modern resonance.

It was also a source of fresh, potable, water.

Sometime after it was made, a nearby river called the Sarasvati breached its banks and flooded the *vav*, filling it with mud. Deprived of a facility that had become so much a part of their lives, the citizens probably appealed to their king. In 1084, the Solankis constructed a major water

A sculpture of Kalki, the avatar of the future.

purification and flood-control structure: the Sahasralinga *Talav*, the Lake of a Thousand *Linga*s.

Leaving the *vav* behind, we drove a short distance, parked our car, and walked through a large, lower-lying, area to the *Talav*. It's an intriguing structure set in a grove of old trees. It is dry now and has only been partially excavated but enough has been unearthed to give a good idea of its original purpose. Water from the Sarasvati was tapped to cascade down an inclined channel into a large, circular, stone-lined pool. The pool's walls were lined with concentric tiers of decreasing size. At right angles to the inlet, there was an outlet. This allowed the water stored in the pool to flow out, after it had reached a level more than half-way up the pool. This water was led into a step-lined canal ending in three circular sluice gates, set side by side. From there it took a sharp right turn before it was held in the main reservoir. The stepped sides of the reservoir held small Shiva shrines and ended in a Shiva temple with a long, covered, forecourt with 48 pillars, stretching down the spine of the reservoir. The massive, high, sanctum of the temple must once have dominated this complex and had probably been crowned by a tower which later collapsed.

The whole hydrological structure covers seven hectares, that is, 17 acres, and had been built by Sidhraj Jaysinh in 1084 during the reign of the aesthetic Solankis.

There are many levels in the beautiful Rani ki Vav.

The scientifically designed sedimentation tank near the Rani ki Vav.

All the tiers of Rani ki Vav have richly sculpted panels.

In the absence of any explanation of the legendary, 'filtration system' we came to our own conclusions.

The circular pond, fed by the river, was constructed to swirl the water around, aerating it and exposing it to sunlight. It also served as a sedimentation tank, allowing suspended particles to settle to the bottom. This pond was probably stocked with carp which fed on insects and algae, further cleaning the water of pests and impurities. The upper surface of this water, the clearest part, was then led off into a long channel filled with living plants such as water hyacinth and strelitzia or ginger lily which absorb

harmful metals and other dangerous substances. These water-loving plants grow rapidly and so the sluice gates were installed to prevent them from clogging the third stage of this filtration system where the water flowed over a bed of charcoal and only then was allowed to enter into the drinking water reservoir sanctified by the Shiva shrines and the great Shiva temple. The water filtered and stored here also charged the underground aquifers, replenishing wells including the monumental Rani ki Vav.

The system which we have imagined is a very old one that has now been successfully revived by environmentalists in other flowing water systems in India. But that is not all.

We also believe that the *talav* and its peripheral lands served another purpose. When the Sarasvati was in spate, and overflowed its banks, these became a balancing factor, the tank with the surrounding lands acting as a flood plain, or shallow lake, to protect the *vav* from inundation. This is why this complex covers a spread of seven hectares and why the pillared forecourt of the Shiva temple has been built in two levels. The twin floors, and the Shivling shrines dotting the steps accessing the *talav*, served as flood gauges giving timely warning of the rising level of the river.

Sadly, with the passing of the Solankis, this knowledge was lost. The Sahasralinga Talav became silted up and lost its flood-controlling effect, and, eventually, the fury of the monsoon-engorged river, poured into the Rani ki Vav filling it with silt, protecting it from would-be marauders and predators. In 1958 it was discovered by the ASI and it began to live again as the amazing historic monument we see today.

There are about 12 *vavs* listed for tourists in Gujarat but two are fairly representative of the intriguing features in these water pavilions. We also visited the 15th century

Carved panels on the Adalaj Vav.

The Adalaj Vav, a well for many reasons.

Adalaj Vav built by the queen of a Vaghela chief. The *vav* shares a common forecourt with a living temple built atop a raised platform to the left and also a common wall with the temple. It was probably part of the *vav* complex but was not taken over by the Archaeological Survey of India.

Built in 1499, in Gujarat's Sultanate era, this *vav* also has some Islamic motifs like the kissing fish at the shaft of the well. The shaft is an octagonal one accessed through spiral staircases carved into the left and right. The pillars, lintels and other parts of this *vav* are also intricately carved but though they are eye-catching they lack the delicacy of Solanki sculptures. Using a torch we were able to discern the depiction of a monarch on a stool: he was probably Virasimha, husband of Rudra who built the Adalaj Vav. There were also dancers and musicians but, by comparison with the Rani ki Vav, the sculptures did not hold our attention. Clearly, the zeal that had inspired the Solanki builders and artisans had diminished by the time the Vaghela chieftains had come to power. Or, perhaps, this had been constructed primarily as a resting place for pilgrims visiting the temple and therefore, did not demand much attention.

Nevertheless, it continues to attract a steady stream of visitors, since it is only 15 kms from Ahmedabad. And it has been doing so for more than 500 years which says much for the continuing allure of these intriguing, sculpted, water pavilions.

The Golden City on a Hill

JAISALMER

The city first noosed us when we were very young in the hand-holding darkness. It was 'Bombay' then. And we were a fledgling Naval family with a scooter and dreams. Was this a dream? The screen brightened and filled with magic. 'Can it be real?' we asked ourselves. 'Or is this a movie set made for Shahrazad, Aladdin and Ali Baba?' This was fantasy unreeling before our eyes. 'Some day,' we promised ourselves, 'we'll go there.'

So we did, along a tan-coloured road where the dust swirled like djinns dancing

As it settled, slowly, a camel and its red-turbaned driver emerged out of the haze. We asked him "Where is Jaisalmer?" He turned and pointed. A sharp wind shredded the dust-cloud, combed the gnarled thorn trees, cleared the air. There, stretching across the blue horizon, was a fort on a hill. It rose high above the flat, desert, floor. Rounded bastions, battlements and high walls of tawny sandstone encircled it, dominating the landscape.

"That is the Sonar Qila," the camel driver said. "The Golden Fort."

The golden battlements of Jaisalmer's Sonar Qila.

The forbidding walls of the Sonar Qila.

We drove down the desert road, this *Arabian Nights* fantasy growing in our vision. At the parking lot, the forbidding yellow walls soared above us. Travellers, peddlers, and vendors mingled in a bazaar-like hubbub and a bearded seller of 'hand-woven rugs'...or so he claimed...could have been offering a Flying Carpet to whisk us away to the highest towers of the fort.

We trudged up ramps built for horses and through narrow, winding lanes, to those eagle heights. Much of the spell of Jaisalmer lies in its history, an ever present incantation from the past that spreads like an invisible net over the city. The foundations were laid in 1156 AD by Maharawal Jaisal and it took seven years to complete. From the height at which we now stood, the founder of this city had had a commanding view of the surrounding countryside and assessed how much 'transit tax' he should levy on the caravans plying between Sind, now in Pakistan, and Delhi. It was a very lucrative business. When the caravans ended with the coming of the railways, Jaisalmer found a new source of revenue. It offered a safe haven for gangs of marauders raiding the rich towns of neighbouring states. Naturally, they paid Protection Money to Jaisalmer!

The swashbuckling legends of brigands and bandits, recounted in the yellowing pages of *The Arabian Nights*, became real-life tales in Jaisalmer.

Fattened by trade and tribute, the princes and merchants of Jaisalmer began to flaunt their prosperity. Space is very restricted in the Fort, and so

A street in Jaisalmer.

the rich and powerful families had to build upwards, and embellish their sandstone buildings with carvings as intricate as frozen lace. We trod through the narrow, man-made canyons of the old town marvelling at oriel windows as delicate as almond icing. Every beautifully carved mansion in Jaisalmer has its own tale to tell. There's the story of the two brothers who created the Nathmalji ki Haveli. The right and left facades are similar, but they are not identical. We examined them carefully and noticed subtle differences in the scalloped arches, the supporting pillars of the balconies, even the flowers carved on the two wings of the main door.

Without such imaginative craftsmanship, the Patwon ki Haveli would have been just another row of apartments. The number five occurs frequently in this long mansion. It was built for five brothers who dealt in five commodities from out of five cities. But, more importantly, thanks to skilled craftsmen, the five buildings of the haveli have become an art gallery of the talents of the sculptors and stone masons of Jaisalmer.

At the end of a narrow lane we discovered the architectural riches of the Jain Temples. They had been built by a determinedly pacifist community of traders who, quite literally, would not even hurt a fly. And yet they thrived in a city of fearsome desert warriors. They expressed their love of the exuberance of the living world in their richly decorated temples. Pillars were covered with superb sculptures and, while walking barefoot amid the

The intricate oriel windows and balconies of Nathmalji ki Haveli.

Equally intriguing monuments lie on the outer fringes of the fort. We walked down a slope, past stubby autorickshaws, to a high gate leading to the rain-fed Gadisar Lake. A courtesan named Telia, a favourite of one of the Rawals, had built it, but the orthodox people of Jaisalmer felt that they would be polluted if they walked through her gate. The ingenious woman then erected a temple to Lord Laxminarayana on the first floor of the gate and asked the citizens if they objected to walking under an idol of the Preserver!
Such legends continue to draw visitors to this fabled city.

throng of worshippers carrying flowers and offerings, we looked up and caught a domed ceiling, flaring with sunlight, and carved like the heart of an enormous flower.

The temples, dedicated to the Jain Tirthankars Rishabdev, Sambhavnath and Parswanath, lie in the crowded heart of the fortified city. Not far from them are a wide flight of steps staging down from a marble throne. This is on one side of the old palace, now seemingly abandoned. Here, on the festival of Dussehra, the ruler and all his court oversaw the sacrifice of animals in honour of the Mother Goddess, Destroyer of Darkness and Evil. Musicians played in the gallery on one side and, on the last day of the festival, a buffalo was taken to the wilderness outside the town, released, and pursued by mounted swordsmen. The one who caught up with the bovine had to cut off its head with a single blow of his sword. These ceremonial sacrifices came to an end when the Princes lost their titles, and much of their incomes, in democratic India. But the open grandstand and marble throne remain as monuments to another age.

We saw both foreigners and domestic tourists pay substantial entrance and camera fees for most of the places visited by them, without batting an eyelid. And the shops and vendors did a roaring trade. We found a peddler near Nathmalji ki Haveli who offered genuine fossilised wood and marine vegetation. One vegetable fossil, we were informed, had the property of turning milk into yoghurt overnight, regardless of the ambient temperature. A Bengali visitor assured us that she had tried it and it was 'Very effective!' The old trading instincts of Jaisalmeris are still alive and flourishing!

We walked the narrow, winding streets threading through the high canyons of houses. Once, possibly, lovelorn maidens stood in oriel windows thrusting out over the street, throwing roses and messages to their lovers waiting below. And then, when moonlight silvered Jaisalmer, and filled deep purple shadows into the canyons, lovers would elope on fleet-footed camels across the haunting dunes of the desert.

But there were also deeper, darker, forces at work in this fairy-tale setting. We always pause and look up at the strangely top-heavy creation of Salim Singh's haveli. Folklorists speak of the legendary wealth of this 19th century merchant prince. His financial clout gave him considerable power over the ruler. In his arrogance, Salim Singh decided that he had to have direct access to the palace rather than be forced to descend to street level. He planned to build a bridge from his mansion, over the city, to the palace: a sort of private fly-over to assert his unchallenged authority over the princes and people of Jaisalmer. Sadly, for him, a new prince ascended the throne and he decided to teach Salim Singh a lesson he would never forget. He had his cannon turned on the rising mansion and blew away its challenging upper floors.

We love the tale, just as we love the stories of Harry Potter, and Hans Andersen and the Disney Studios.

The town's heritage also survives in more contemporary, colourful, ways. On the wall leading up to the fortified city, puppeteers displayed their traditional moving dolls: princes and princesses, snake charmers and wizards and kings with plumed turbans. Puppetry is a living, growing, folk-theatre in Rajasthan and we've seen the colourful puppets of this heraldic land decorate many sophisticated homes all across India. According to one of the puppet makers, they are hot favourites with honeymooners: "They always buy a pair because it reminds them of their wedding day!"

Salim Singh's ambitious haveli.

Sam's Dunes.

A little out of Jaisalmer we opted for the unique desert experience of Sam's Dunes. Literally hundreds of saddled camels, and a few camel carts, line up at the side of the road, awaiting customers. Riding on a camel is a rather undulating and orchestrated experience: 'music' courtesy the camels. These 'ships of the desert' complain as a matter of in-bred principle. They groan when asked to sit, groan when commanded to stand; they groan when they start walking and also when asked to stop. And when they galumph…which is the best description of their swaying walk…the spines of their riders get an excellent exercise: better than swaying in a rocking chair.

But, in spite of all this, a camel ride through the scrub desert was a great experience. As the scrub thinned out and the dunes began to rise ahead, hordes of colourfully-dressed dancers, singers and musicians ran out to greet each new batch of visitors. They offered us our own, personal, entertainment when we dismounted from our humped steeds, sat on a convenient dune, and watched the drama of sunset on Sam's Dunes.

Puppets on a fortress wall.

A Kalbelia dancer, as sinuous as the snakes they charm.

Then, as the sun descended lower and still lower on the frozen waves of sand, the dunes turned saffron, russet, rose-pink, briefly scarlet and deep crimson, before the shadows started to creep up from the troughs and cover the crests, and the bright stars came out above.

Many visitors returned to their hotels after that but we trudged down to a campfire flaming on a packed-earth circular stage, while folk musicians played on their traditional wind, string and percussion instruments. Then, out of the shadows, came the brightly dressed Kalbelia dancers. Officially they are called 'gypsy dancers': perhaps that sounds more romantic than saying that they belong to the tribe of traditional snake charmers. Judging by the lissom grace of their swift movements it is quite likely that they have learnt many of their sinuous motions from the serpents that their people have been performing with for generations.

Then again, coming to think of it, the gypsies of Europe, the so-called 'Romanies', believe that they migrated from India, many generations ago.

In Andalusia we sat through a performance of Flamenco dancers in an auditorium. But for all their power and precision, they did not transport us to another world and another time as the Kalbelia dancers did, when they spun around a blazing campfire under the bright desert stars in the mysterious dunes of Sam.

And then, once more, we were sitting in the hand-holding dark while the wide-screen of our minds filled with the images of that city on a hill rising out of the desert, wreathed in the swirling legends of its magical past.

The Evolution of Gods

THE MYSTIQUE OF FOLK HEROES

In Rajasthan the truth stood out dramatically.

India is not a melting pot, we are a mosaic. Over the millennia, all the races of the earth have migrated into India and become Indians. But even when they have shaped their social behaviour to fit in with the other pieces in the jigsaw, they have retained their essential individuality often centred around their own folk heroes, as we discovered.

From the princely city of Bikaner we drove out to visit the most unusual folk deity of them all. Karni Mata was reputedly born in 1387, in a cave, in Deshnok. She belonged to the *Charan* tribe. Today, a white temple has been built around the cave and the priests in that shrine are *Charans*. They believe that their souls, between successive rebirths, are held in the bodies of rats. Hordes of rats scamper about this temple, dine on huge metal plates

Furred guests of the goddess Karni Mata.

The sanctuary of Karni Mata.

placed on the floor, and live in a warren of holes in the walls of the shrine. The *Charans* say that any visitor who sees an albino rat has been particularly blessed by Karni Mata. We've seen two of them.

Much of the lore associated with such folk icons is oral and so is likely to be embellished at every telling. Consequently, the vast body of scripture associated with better-established divinities tends to overwhelm the bardic version. The written word is more permanent, easier to enforce, than the verbal one. This absorption into orthodoxy has almost overtaken Karni Mata. Though her image is still identifiable, she is being increasingly considered to be a manifestation of the benign, lion-mounted, Mother Goddess, Durga.

A similar transformation is connected with the mother of Jeen Mata. She was a beautiful nymph whose clothes were stolen by Gangoji, a governor of Dhandu, while she was bathing in a pond. The celestial maiden agreed to marry the governor provided that he could never enter her room unannounced. Sadly, he did so after they had had five children. To his horror he found his wife in her real form: a formidable lioness. She vanished, taking three of their children with her. Jeen and her brother were left back on earth. After Jeen had been married for some years, she had a disagreement with her husband, left him, and wandered as a mendicant in the Aravalli Mountains. There, after many austerities, she became a manifestation of the Mother Goddess. The temple erected to her still stands in Jeen in Sikar district to the north-west of Jaipur.

Increasingly, however, her Mother Goddess aspect is being emphasised and her folk heroine aspect is fading away.

While the legends woven around folk heroes, and retold over the generations, are often vague about dates, many folklorists have told us that the majority of Rajasthan's folk heroes lived during the reign of the Mughal Emperor Aurangzeb. The 17th century saw a wave of religious intolerance sweep over the world: Aurangzeb was a contemporary of England's Oliver Cromwell. Both were affected by bouts of bigotry, giving rise to folk heroes who opposed them.

One of these religious leaders was Sidh Rustomji. Legend has it that Aurangzeb was annoyed by the miracles of Sidh Rustomji and ordered a huge pit filled with burning coals. Undeterred, Sidh Rustomji stepped into it naked and emerged unharmed, clothed, with a melon in one hand and a corn cob in the other. Aurangzeb was so astounded that he gave permission to the Sidh's followers to perform their fire-walking rituals. We saw one and were amazed at the sight of devotees dancing in the fire pit, even holding glowing coals in their mouths, unharmed. Recent research has indicated a strange empathy between the fire walkers and the other devotees who surround the pit, urging them on. The heart rates of both the firewalkers and the spectators seem to beat at the same pace as if their emotional link had, suddenly, become a physical one.

Ramdeoji, one of Rajasthan's folk heroes.

The interaction of faiths occurs frequently in the legends of Rajasthan's folk heroes. Ramdeoji, according to legend, was born only after his father had made a pilgrimage to Lord Krishna's shrine in Dwarka, Gujarat. His followers still consider him to be an incarnation of Krishna. He also, however, has an Islamic presence. Once, so the story goes, five Muslim savants from Mecca came to test Ramdeoji's powers. They claimed that they could not dine with him because they had left their utensils in Arabia. Miraculously, Ramdeoji produced their bowls. Ever since then, we were assured, Ramdeoji has also been known as Ram Shah *Pir* and is venerated by Muslims. When we visited his principal shrine in Ramdeora village, 13 kms from Pokran, a van full of bearded Muslim men drew up. Sadly, we forgot to ask them if they were devotees of the *Pir*.

We've not heard any songs being sung about Ramdeoji, though, given the rich folk-entertainment tradition of Rajasthan, we have probably missed such recitals. But we do know that one folk hero has created an interesting tradition of wandering bards: Pabuji. He was a warrior of the martial Rathore clan. Pabuji's sense of duty led him to abandon his bride at the wedding ceremony to gallop to the aid of a widow. The old lady's favourite blind calf had been stolen by brigands. Sadly, Pabuji died fighting the marauders.

This romantic tale is just one of the legends of Pabuji sung by wandering Bhopa musicians. In cool desert evenings, village people invite Bhopas to entertain them. When they have assembled, a little after dusk, the Bhopas slowly unfurl their *pad*, a 10-metre long scroll brightly painted with the heroic exploits of their folk hero. The Bhopa sings the ballad of Pabuji, accompanying himself on the stringed *Ravan Hatha*, while his wife holds an oil lamp and dances, identifying each unfolding episode on the *pad*. In spite of the increasing reach of the TV, the Bhopa-ballads still attract people, drawn to the tales of their valiant ancestor.

The legendary Pabuji.

The folk hero with the most lasting impact on the environment of Rajasthan is, undoubtedly, Jambeshwar. We learnt about him quite by accident.

The landscape of the desert areas of Rajasthjan is sere and harsh. Dramatic dunes spread, relieved only by long lines of brightly-dressed women, their gleaming brass or dull ochre terracotta pots on their heads. Theirs is a daily trudge for water. Occasionally, the sand gives way to sun-baked soil, cracked and parched, dotted with a few clumps of thorny cactus or desert shrubs that seldom grow into trees: the pressure on them is too much, particularly if there is a village nearby. Village kitchens need firewood and so the trees around a village become fewer and fewer.

But one year, when we were driving through this starkly beautiful, but inhospitable landscape, we saw a blur of green. Curious, we drove towards it and discovered that it was village in a cooling grove of trees. The greening began far on the outskirts of the village. Grass spread out from the first bushes dotted around the village. The thorn scrub merged into thickets; the thickets grew into groves; the groves gave way to large trees. The men and women were tall and handsome. To our amazement, we saw peafowl, partridge and chinkara deer wandering fearlessly around the village. We also spotted blackbuck grazing with their cattle. This green miracle in the desert belonged to the Bisnois: the followers of a creed of 29, *bis-noi*, principles laid down by a visionary herdsman. That was more than 500 years before 'The Environment' became a fashionable buzz-word.

We sat on a *khatia* in the dappled shade of the village, sipped glasses of milk thick with yellow cream, and were told the tale of their folk-hero turned deity: Jambeshwar.

He was born in a little Rajasthani village in 1451. As was the custom in those days, it was his job to take his family's herds out to graze. There wasn't much fodder, or many grazing lands, but the observant Jambeshwar noticed that wherever the thorn trees spread their sparse shade, grass grew and survived the scorching sun of this arid land. He also saw that when the trees acted as wind-breaks, the droppings left by his herds, chinkara deer and blackbuck, fertilised the land, causing more grass to grow. Otherwise, the wind blew everything away and the land became arid again. The young herds-boy began to appreciate the self-renewing cycle of nature which binds all living things into an inter-dependent web. If he could use this web, the whole land would be greened.

This is the basic story we've heard repeated by many people who claimed that they knew the legends surrounding this remarkable man. But as he looked after his herds during those long days in the desert other insights came to him. If trees protected the land then green trees shouldn't be cut. Therefore only deadwood should be removed. But there might be little creatures in that wood, so such timber should be washed to remove the insects that might be hiding in it. Meat, of course, was anathema; so was dirt of any sort: everyone should bathe every morning, filter water through a cloth, and wear white so that you could see any living creature that might have taken shelter in your clothes.

Out of his observations were born the Twenty Nine Principles that, eventually, became the precepts of a new, environmental, faith. Consequently, his followers came to be called the Bis-nois, the 'Twenty-niners'. Jambeshwar is now referred to as Jamboji.

Later, we were told that many of the Bisnois believe that they could be reincarnated as blackbuck and so they are particularly protective of these animals. As a forest guard expressed it: "No one dares to hunt or fell wood within the zone of protection of a Bisnoi village."

There are tales of wood-be hunters who have been pulled out of their jeeps and forced to walk for hours. "And," added a knowledgeable Forest Officer, "if you're caught killing or wounding an animal, you're likely to have an accident!"

In keeping with their life-respecting faith, the Bisnois are strict vegetarians and they do not keep goats and sheep. "If we don't kill," we were told, "why should we breed animals for others to kill? We are strictly cattle herds-people and our animals are kept only for their milk."

"How prosperous can a milk-based economy be, in Rajasthan?" we asked a district official.

"Very prosperous," he said, "if you're a Bisnoi."

Jambeshwar, folk hero turned deity of the Bisnois.

It sounded too good to be true and, with the onslaught of ideas in our Age of Information, the old ways are bound to be eroded. But, at least for the present, the Twenty-Niners seem to have retained their sane way of life.

Driving out of Bisnoi-country we fell into line behind three powerful motor-cycles roaring down the road ahead of us, like outriders. When all our efforts to overtake them failed we asked why there was so much traffic on this rural road. Our guide grinned and said: "Look at the cans mounted on both sides of their carriers."

Large zinc canisters were clamped on their bikes, like strange rocket-launchers. "Those Harley-Davidsons are milk delivery vehicles," he added. "Bisnois, of course. They're carrying milk to the markets of Jodhpur."

Obviously, this unique environmental religion pays and, like Jamboji, our gods are still evolving.

Fair of the Brightest Moon

PUSHKAR

All over Rajasthan, the tribes began to move.

They had seen the moon fattening for the brightest night of the year and had started their trek. There were camel-herding Raikars, with turbans like smouldering sunsets, and nomadic Gujjars with long staves across their shoulders, herding their lowing cattle. Itinerant Lohars…those remarkable blacksmiths, bound by an ancient oath never to live under a permanent roof…plodding besides their creaking, nail-studded, bullock-cart homes. Also martial Bhils whose brigand ancestors had haunted the scrub-covered ravines but now, they assured us, they were horse trainers, horse breeders and more: "We taught the world to play polo!" Then there were the women, laughing and gossiping in clannish groups, their full skirts swaying like blossoms in a breeze, jewellery clinking and flashing in the autumn sun.

Once, there had been such fairs in medieval Europe, but they had been overwhelmed by migrations to the cities and the absorption of the tribes in the anonymity of the great metropolises. Thankfully, Pushkar remains.

Following the tribes, we drove out of Ajmer, through the settling dust of the caravans' passage heading, as they had, for the brassy desert around

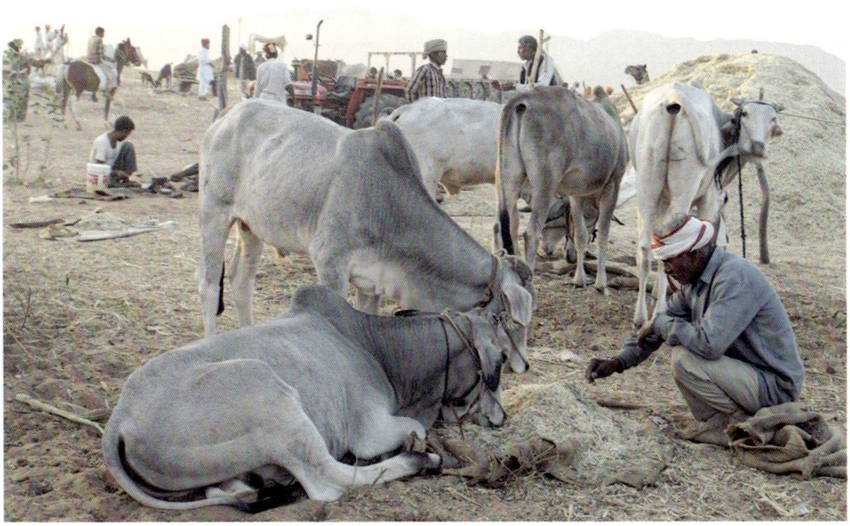

Pushkar is a major cattle fair.

the three sacred lakes of Pushkar. A legendary time ago, Lord Brahma, the Creator of the Hindu Trinity, had flown over this land. Three petals had fallen from the lotus he carried and touched the earth below. Miraculously, three lakes had appeared: *Kanishtha* Pushkar, the youngest; *Madhyam* Pushkar, the middle one; and the great elder, *Jyeshtha* Pushkar. Recognising this as an auspicious omen, the Creator had landed and performed a powerful fire sacrifice. Ever since then, people have gathered here in their thousands to bathe and worship on the anniversary of the Creator's sacrifice.

Over the centuries, Pushkar has grown into a heady mix of faith, festivities and hard-headed haggling.

Its magic unfolded at dusk as our car breasted a hill. In the distance glinted the three lakes, their stepped shores rising to the massed old town of Pushkar: flat-roofed in shades of yellow and white. And through the soft ochre haze, campfires twinkled on the plain, each fire marking the resting caravan of a family, a community, a tribe, with their animals tethered around them.

We honked and manoeuvred our way through crowded roads lined with shops, and blaring with music, into the comparative serenity of the Village set up by the state's Tourism Development Corporation. We slept early, had breakfast while desert-dew still sparkled on the plain, then hurried across the road, and into the vibrancy of the fair.

Suddenly, the future and the past don't exist and every experience is etched permanently in the present like an indelible succession of freeze-frames. Even a dromedary's plodding tread.

We jink, instinctively, out of a camel's path touched by its acrid aroma; turn swiftly to frame a smiling face; look away from a fearsome mendicant. He grins and warns, "You're shooting into the sun. You might damage your exposure meter with overload!" His accent is guttural Indo-Germanic. Pushkar attracts an eclectic mix of people.

Through the bustling, milling, crowds of shoppers and gapers and jugglers and hustlers, bemused Caucasians stand out like exotic weeds in a garden of wild flowers, wafting expensive after shaves and French perfumes. They are attired in Marks & Sparks outfits for the tropics: wide-brimmed hats, khakis, desert boots, Calvin Klein shades and binoculars.

Visitors on a camel tour of the fair.

Campers cook their dinner.

Camels at a drinking trough.

The disciplined South Asian groups mince past in bowing, smiling, camera-clicking uniformity behind their umbrella-lofting guide speaking in sing-song cadences. And surging through the crowd, like the prow of a Viking long-ship, a giant bearded Scandinavian, burnt nut-brown by the sun, comes striding like a goliath in a green lungi and a saffron kurta with *Hari Krishna Hari Ram* printed all over. Olaf Odinson, Reykjavik: that's what he has inscribed on a silver identity bracelet engraved by an itinerant silversmith equipped with a metal stool, an attaché case and a small electric drill with a long, frayed, cable leading into a shop selling CDs and cassettes. The Scandinavian wants meditative chants by Enigma, or Sufi music. He strides on when he's offered Bollywood remixes instead. Where will the developed world find its catharsis when Pushkar is bulldozed by 'progress' and bland high-rises mushroom where the variegated tribes now gather? For the present, however, it is still as alive and bewildering as a twirling kaleidoscope.

The bustling, central, area of the fair is a jostling mass of visitors thronging, entertainment booths, eateries. The farmers and their animals are dotted on the dun-coloured plain all around. That's the trading pit of the fair, redolent of camps and cooking fires. We decide to visit it later: it's midday and we're hungry. The irresistible aroma of frying pakoras and sizzling, succulent, golden jalebis nooses out from a dhaba presided over by a man who has the build of a wrestler and the expression of a jovial buccaneer. His high-calorie snack sharpens our perceptions. A man lies near a spiked pile of pitchforks, called *chaukni*, a mobile phone plastered to his ear. Pushkar bridges time and equipment: *chaukni* and cell-phone perfectly matched.

A vendor of wooden rakes relaxes with a mobile phone.

Lethal hardware for a desert warrior.

Belu Ram sits in front of a flashing armoury of swords, daggers, jack-knives, stilettos and other variations of lethal slicing weapons. Swords are so much a part of the Rajasthani psyche that a tourism brochure once carried the title *Blood, Blades and Chivalry*. Images of legendary Samurai, Junkers and the Three Musketeers flash through our minds. Here, however, swords are not the stuff of legends: they are an essential part of everyday life. We recall seeing a groom in a turban and a business suit hefting a sword as he escorted his bejewelled bride back from a temple.

We leave Belu Ram as a whipcord-slim septuagenarian calls for a curved sword and examines it very carefully.

We drift through the crowd, applaud the camel races and turban-tying competitions, thrill at the roaring tension of the Well of Death, delight at children tumbling out of an inflatable Mickey Mouse. We visit a tent with superb white horses with pink ears. A young Haryanvi farmer has himself photographed beside the tallest and most expensive of the steeds the way a Formula 1 fan might stand beside a Ferrari. He says that the superb animal was of the *Nukra* breed and that it had originally been sold for 13 lakhs but was now priced at 51 lakhs. He is convinced that the owner does not really want to sell it but has put a price tag on it only to attract attention to his other horses.

We move on, deluged by sights and sounds, textures, aromas and flavours, gritty with the dust of a myriad moving feet and hooves and wheels, saturated with experiences. We sit for a while at the stall of a cane-juice vendor, sip glasses of energy-boosting green syrup. A cane crusher spins and a bell tinkles and long stalks of sugar-cane are fed in at one end and pulp emerges at the other as the sap gushes into a jug. A 40s-going-on-20s man, in a Harvard crimson t-shirt and a brown stubble, eyes our obvious enjoyment with wariness and asks, "Is it safe?" We smile blandly at him.

Children enjoying a Mickey Mouse slide.

Tribal shoppers at a trinket shop.

"Is a double-burger with French fries and a coke safe?" He grins, shrugs and orders a tall glass of *ganna*-juice. Will our juice-vendor's name appear in *Lonely Planet*?

It is only then that we notice the lengthening shadows and realise that we have been here the whole day. We stroll past women shopping for bangles while their lone male companion stands behind, frowning unhappily. Camels

A rural skit where men dress as sheep.

slurp water from a trough, dipping into their own reflections. The great tented camp on the plain, and its cooking fires, mottle the dusk, touched by the orange disc of the setting sun. When we pick our way through them, many families look up, smile, and offer to share their meal with us: charcoal baked bajra *rotlas* and lightly fried beans of a desert shrub with a delicately bitter flavour, accompanied by a brass tumbler of *chaas*, a yoghurt drink spiced with chillies. Most desert people have a strong tradition of hospitality. We sit cross-legged around a fire, on soft sheepskin rugs, listen to a man with luxuriant moustaches play a twanging mouth-harp, smile at their near awe when they learn we live in the Himalayas. We return to our Tourist Village and take in an amusing rural play about two women trying to drive reluctant cattle; men play the driven beasts much to the delight of the audience.

We rise before dawn the next morning and merge into a river of humanity flowing towards the *Jyeshtha* Pushkar. We are caught in an irresistible current for almost an hour. We can't slow down; we can't speed up; we can't move right or left. Then people begin peeling off and veering into lanes that lead down to their favourite bathing ghats. Placing ourselves on the flat roof of a lake-side temple, we look around. What an incredible sight!

On three sides spreads the *Jyeshtha* Pushkar Lake, metallic in the pre-dawn light. The steps leading down to the lake are crowded with bare-chested

The sanctum of Lord Brahma.

The great bathing ritual.

BABA RESTAURANT

men and brightly dressed women. All eyes are fixed on the glowing, eastern, horizon. And then, as a chip of the sun thrusts over the edge, the temple bells begin to ring. Men and women plunge into the water, chants surge out from a thousand throats as the bathers raise water in their cupped hands and let it fall as a libation to the sun and a new day. Priests wade into the bathing pilgrims carrying brass thalis containing coconuts, rice, vermilion powder and roses. Soon, a floating carpet of pink rose petals starts to spread out from the bathing ghats across the lake.

Later that morning, we tread carefully along the water-slicked streets, turn down a lane full of saddles for horses and camels and follow the pilgrims as they climb the steps of one of the very few Brahma temples in our land. The steps are divided by a railing, the left of the steps are for those going up, the right for those returning. Further on, the jostling crowd is again divided: men on the right, women on the left. The inner sanctum of the temple is encased in a frame of embossed silver. The idol of the Creator seems to have three heads looking right, left and forward. All three heads are crowned and the crown on the central head has a high dome much like the one worn formally by the Pope. On the right of the idol is another of his consort, Saraswati, goddess of wisdom and learning, identified with the great, vanished, river of the early Aryans. Both idols have polished stone eyes which glitter. One religious tradition contends that it is only after the eyes have been inserted into an image that the statue becomes an idol worthy of worship. We ask the priest in attendance if this is the belief here but he is too busy ministering to worshippers to answer us.

That night, while the great full moon of autumn silvers the lake, we stand on our temple terrace and look out over the water. Thousands of tiny oil lamps flicker like gold fireflies on the steps of the ghats. Slowly, while temple bells chime and incense rises in fragrant blue clouds, pilgrims carry their lamps to the water's edge and set them afloat in homage to a lake of the Creator.

We know that, when dawn comes, bright and flaming over the desert, most of the lamps would have flickered out, and the pilgrims and their camels and cattle and caravans will be streaming back across the sands.

But next autumn, before the huge *Purnima* moon brightens the sky, the tribes will trudge back, lured by the irresistible spell of Pushkar.

Tales of the Painted Havelis

SHEKHAWATI

Every town in Shekhawati is an art gallery.

Particularly the historic town of Mandawa, in the heart of Shekhawati. The paintings appeared everywhere. All down the narrow streets, where camel-carts plodded, the old havelis rose: mansions with arched windows and pillars and balconies. And every available flat surface was alive with murals. There were bright paintings of Rajasthani dowagers and damsels peeping out from heavy elephant carriages. Then there was the monstrous *Chungi Chiriya*, a bird which would have made Sinbad's Roc look like a house sparrow. It had picked up a brace of elephants in the talons of each gigantic foot, ensnared them with its anaconda-like tail and was crushing them in its gargantuan beak.

On other walls, gods, goddesses, demons and sundry immortal beings made war or love or, generally, disported themselves. Along with the

A painted ceiling in Shekhawati.

Glowing in gold leaf, a panel celebrates Lord Shiva.

incidents drawn from our folklore, there were also whimsical vignettes of the British era. Men with moustaches and solar topis were a repetitive theme. One rode a strange cycle with pedals on the front wheel, and a party of them went hunting with shotguns and riding boots. Above a long line of shops, a train chugged past, along with a guard waving a flag rather cheerily. Another wall held a father and son in the typical black caps and coats of the traders raising their right hands and pointing to a curious contraption identified as an *Urnewala Jahaz*, a Flying Machine.

Occasionally, the owners of the great mansions had had themselves immortalised. In the front of one haveli, a prosperous merchant had been portrayed sitting in a chair in a tile-floored room complete with a curtained window, marble-topped table, a vase of flowers, a book and an umbrella. Even the old Dutch masters had not captured the smug, self-satisfied, burgher ideal more effectively.

And yet, all these soaring mansions, radiating the epitome of the prosperous traders' domestic aspirations, were deserted. They slumbered, crumbling slowly in the desert sun, while decrepit chowkidars sat on sagging *khatia*s and dreamed of the days when Shekhawati had been the bustling hub of the caravan trade.

From the mid-1800s to the 1930s, Shekhawati had prospered, and had been protected by the descendants of the warrior who gave his name to the town: Rao Shekhaji. His Castle Mandawa still stands and his descendants host visitors in the old, regal, style.

European hunters and a strange cycle on a damaged wall.

A mural of summer—a train, women on swings and hunters.

A diorama of a traditional kitchen.

A diorama of the accountant in his office; a fan-puller in the foreground.

We drove over to the Castle Mandawa to learn more about the life and times of this old, painted, town. A senior member of the former princely family explained: "Our *qilas*, our castles, had a big gate, four towers or more and a number of other features to distinguish them from other dwellings." Their halls were embellished with painted walls bright with mirror-work, enamel and gold leaf. Quite naturally, when the traders of the town grew prosperous, they wanted their homes to be as resplendent. In the castle, we met the very dignified Kirpal Singh, a traditional mural artist who works, occasionally, in Mandawa Castle. He said, "My ancestors were told 'Paint what you like', for the owners of the havelis were too busy to tell them what to paint, 'but make sure that it is better than the murals of any other haveli.' So, naturally, we chose a wide variety of subjects and used our imagination. We applied the plaster. Then we covered it with a poison to keep away the lizards who would dirty the paintings. After that we spread a powder of mother-of-pearl or marble to give it a smooth surface. Then we put the white of egg and polish. And then we did the actual paintings: russet brown from bark, green from leaves, yellow from cow's urine, blue from a stone, red from a cactus flower. So then, it was ready."

The murals that emerged were an eclectic mix of observation, skill and fantasy, and the burgeoning bourgeoisie were delighted. Their eye-catching painted mansions proclaimed to the passing caravans that they had arrived,

The courtyard of Castle Mandawa.

A uniformed guard in Castle Mandawa.

spreading the message of their success to the far corners of their commercial world. Their mansions were their huge, self-indulgent, billboards.

But when the British began to web India with their railway lines, the caravan routes withered away. The havelis could no longer advertise the trading families' achievements to the world. The intrepid entrepreneurs moved away to greener pastures: the commercial cities of Bombay, Calcutta and even Singapore.

Interestingly, however, the railways had also given them their unique identity. In those early days, according to the senior member of the family who owns Mandawa Castle, when the trading families first moved out of this desert area, "The railways went only as far as Jodhpur in Marwar. When anyone in the big trading cities asked where they were going, they said 'Marwar'. So everyone dressed as they were began to be called Marwaris."

At first, the great 'Marwari' families like the Birlas, Poddars, Dalmias, Singhanias and Goenkas made fortunes in their adopted cities, lived frugally, sent money back to their home towns, established welfare schemes for their community, and continued to embellish their havelis more out of tradition than purpose. Occasionally, they returned to their old mansions to celebrate festivals and special family events and then the havelis were spruced up and, possibly, the murals were retouched. But, as the years wore on, and new generations were born, the tug of the old mansions diminished. The doors of the mansions were locked and sealed and in the courts where the families had made enormous fortunes, the chowkidars strung their drying lines, cooked their food, covered the bright old murals with soot and grime.

When we left the town of the painted mansions, on that first trip, we believed that here was a 'Marwari' heritage crying out to be saved, before the wind and the sun and the sand and neglect, erased the fading murals forever. But we admitted that there was no commercially viable reason to save them.

Then, much later, we returned to the Shekawati area in a renovated old train called *The Heritage on Wheels*. Our fellow passengers were, largely, foreigners and we had prepared ourselves to explain to them how we Indians, too, had to be pragmatic and, sometimes, sacrifice our heritage for 'progress' as many countries in the west had done. We left our train and drove in a coach into the dusty old town of Mehnsar. And there, in the Shivbaksh Rai Poddar Haveli, we heaved a sigh of relief. It is also called the Sona Chandi *Saal* or the Gold and Silver office or shop or rest-room. The word *saal*, according to our guide Niranjan Singh Shekhawat, could mean any one of the three. In this case it probably meant all of them.

The whole *saal* was a glittering tribute to the muralists' skills.

We were shown a small, and very insignificant, door which an intruder would, normally, have ignored. It led to a cellar where the family secreted its valuables. And, as if to draw attention away from this subterranean strong-room, was the brilliance and intricacy of the murals, many glittering with gold and silver. There was an entire ceiling which looked like a glowing Persian carpet. A bird's eye view of a fortified and moated city took up another panel. Alcoves carried large religious paintings, one of a rather portly and benign Shiva with Parvati by his side and Ganesh looking up at him lovingly. There were stylised flowers and abstract designs running around the walls or serving as frames for other pictures. Everything glowed as if it had all been painted yesterday. In fact though many of the murals had remained untouched from the time that they had first been created by artists, or so we were told, a large number of them had been restored very recently. It was the same in Dunlod, another town of painted havelis.

In Dunlod, however, the haveli of Arjun Das Goenka had also been turned into a museum of the lifestyle of the age in which it had been built. Statues of an accountant sitting at his low desk, with debtors squatting before him, had been set up exactly where the accounts' office would have been at the height of the old, caravan trade. So were life-size models of a servant grinding grain, yoked cattle in their stall, and a horse-drawn coach. Within the house the murals depicted religious themes and they also seemed to have been touched up recently.

We asked one of the local folk who had followed us in, if a heritage society had been at work. He shook his head. "No," he replied, "the reason is far more pragmatic: money." We looked at him, surprised. "Yes," he repeated. "Hard cash." He nodded towards the manager of the *Heritage on Wheels*. "When the owners learnt that the train would bring in affluent tourists, and that they could charge a fee to allow them to enter their havelis, they realised what a gold mine they were sitting on. They brought in the restorers, threw open their mansions, and have never looked back!" Successful traders can always see the main chance. It seemed fitting that the railway, which had led to the decline of the painted havelis, was now reviving them.

After years of slumbering in the sun, the mural-rich mansions of Shekhawati are, at long last, waking up and smelling the paint.

Shrine of the Great Dervish

AJMER'S DARGAH SHARIF

There is the man and there is all that has grown around him.

At the end of a crowded, and often grimy street, was what has grown around him. It is magnificent. Over more than eight centuries, conquerors and emperors, kings, savants and humble pilgrims have contributed to the growth of a superb complex built around the tomb of one man. Great gates soar and glitter with decorations, pillared halls spread, serene mosques rise, and there is an auditorium, a langar *khana* where great quantities of food are distributed to the poor twice a day, a tank dedicated to the memory of Queen Mary, grandmother of Queen Elizabeth II, and two enormous metal cauldrons in which a fascinating ceremony occurs.

At the heart of this elaborate dargah rises the Mazaar Sharif with a crowned dome above the tomb of Hazrat Khwaja Moinuddin Hasan Chisty. He is also known as Garib Nawaz, Benefactor of the Poor.

We joined a jostling, elbowing, crowd eager to enter the confines of the shrine. In the centre, sequestered by a rope barrier, was a tomb covered

Crowds stream through a narrow road to the Dargah Sharif.

in a deep green chaddar. Our guide's burly nephew raised the edge of the covering, placed it on our heads, and mumbled a prayer, presumably seeking the blessings of the Muslim saint. And then we were out in the open again.

Muslim and Hindu devotees predominated, the women of the desert clans in their bright costumes, their embroidery and jewellery catching the sun. We also noticed two shaven-headed young men in the strawberry robes of Buddhist monks. There was a scattering of foreigners, all soberly dressed, all listening to their guides with great attention.

"This building, with its façade brilliantly decorated with intricate gold designs, is the *mazaar*, the cenotaph of Jahanara Begum, the daughter of

Emperor Shahjahan. Those women, sitting behind the railing, are waiting to ask those two men sitting at the desks to accept their donations for prayers to be said at this cenotaph. Here, only the *khadims*, the descendants of the male companions of the saint, may offer prayers,"

"Why is that?" asked one of his tour group. "Why can't anyone pray?"

The guide looked at her and smiled. "In your church, madam...you said you were a Catholic...don't you ask the priest to offer prayers for you at the altar during Mass? And isn't every Catholic altar virtually a tomb because it holds the relics of saints?" He paused but she said nothing. "It is so, here. You can offer prayers anywhere on your own. But there would be a dangerous stampede if every devotee was allowed to enter the shrine and stay there long enough to pray...It is only a matter of crowd-control and the safety of the pilgrims."

It was indeed an extremely logical explanation.

We walked around, through the crowds, admiring the many structures erected by the devotees of Khwaja Moinuddin Chisty. The two vast cauldrons, the *degs*, had been given by Mughal Emperor Akbar and his son, the Emperor Jehangir. The *degs*, which can hold a fragrant, sweet, porridge of 4,800 kgs and 2,400 kgs respectively, sit on their own fireplaces and are accessed by steps. Devotees who wish to make Ajmer's Dargah this special offering fill the cauldrons with rice, water, sugar, ghee, desiccated fruit and nuts, and saffron and allow it to cook for hours. When it is ready, drummers walk the streets of Ajmer announcing that the food is about to be distributed. Then, after allowing the porridge to cool

One of the great cauldrons dwarfs visitors.

Roses are an acceptable offering at the dargah.

sufficiently, but with steam still rising from the cauldrons, servers jump in and start scooping out the delectable offering and handing it to devotees as a blessing.

Sadly this did not happen when we visited the dargah.

In a corner of the dargah we did, however, find a small tomb linked with a charming legend. This was the tomb of a water carrier, a *bhisti*. Even in this day of centralised plumbing, we have seen these men carrying buffalo-skin sacks filled with water. The story goes that once, when the Emperor Humayun was fleeing from his enemies he came to a river. There was no boat and no bridge to cross. But when he saw a *bhisti* filling his sack with water, he persuaded him to fill the sack with air. Using it as a float, the emperor paddled his way across and evaded his pursuers. As a reward to the *bhisti*, he permitted him to occupy his imperial throne for a day, and even to strike his own leather coins. The water carrier's name was Nizam Sikkah.

This tomb and all the other structures in the Dargah Sharif, Ajmer, are the tangible heritage inspired by the man known as Khwaja Garib Nawaz. But equally important, many would say far more important, is his intangible

The impressive entrance to the tomb of the great Sufi saint.

heritage: his reach as a Sufi seer. We probed into this aspect of his life and uncovered some fascinating and very far reaching beliefs.

Moinuddin Chisty was born in eastern Iran in 1138-39 AD. He was orphaned when he was sixteen and inherited an orchard and a windmill. One day a man dressed in woollen robes called *suf*, came into his orchard and sat in the shade of a tree. These garments usually identified the Islamic mystics who were also known as 'the poor' or *fuqara*, the plural of the Arabic *faqir*. The Persians called them *dervish*. When the young Chisty saw this poor mystic resting in the shade of a tree, he offered him water and grapes from his orchard. The Sufi thanked him and then, taking something out of his robes, he chewed it,

Above: Islamic caps for sale in the shopping arcade of the dargah. Left: The mausoleum of the revered mystic.

Grave of the water carrier who became an emperor for a day.

took the wad out of his mouth, and offered it to Chisty. Unhesitatingly, the boy put it into his own mouth…

We do not know what the substance was but, suddenly, he began to see things in a new light. Some say that it was a symbolic act to test Chisty's resolve to renounce the world and its prejudices and seek spiritual illumination. Others contend that it was a leaf with psychedelic properties still chewed by some Arabian people. The identity of the substance is not important. The fact is, that after that encounter, the mystic is said to have claimed that Moinuddin Chisty had stepped onto the path of enlightenment and that he must now train his mystic powers by finding his own spiritual guide. Chisty sold his orchard and windmill and began to travel around the Islamic world seeking the right mentor.

At that time, Islam had become a rather rigid, conformist faith controlled by a growing body of rules and regulations churned out by religious lawyers. They were much like the Sadducees and Pharisees of Jesus' day who demanded a strict adherence to the written word of the Bible and frowned on others' beliefs. Sufism was a natural reaction to this unbending view of a faith that had come to the Prophet Mohammed by a revelation, not by a static adherence to shibboleth. Islam was ready for the internal revolution that all major religions have to face.

After studying under Sufi savants in the major centres of the Muslim world, Moinuddin Chisty arrived in Ajmer in 1190. He was 52 years old. Clearly his message of a direct and very personal, experience of his creator was exactly what people had been waiting for. While adhering to the tenets of the Holy Koran, the Khwaja and his Chisty brotherhood projected a more humane, less orthodox, image of their faith. A direct fall-out of such heterodox views was the conversion of large swathes of Indians oppressed by the practices of other strictly stratified religions, Moreover, even though. hyper orthodox Islamic pedants frown on such 'frivolities' as music, the Chistiyahs inspired the classical Islamic music of India, particularly the soulful Indo-Pakistani form now known as Sufi music.

Thus, more than 800 years after this gentle mystic came to Ajmer, his intangible heritage continues to build bridges of hope between nations.

The Fortress of Pleasure

MANDU

On a road through Madhya Pradesh, the opening lines kept ringing in our minds.

The Afghan came down like the wolf on the fold
And his cohorts were gleaming in purple and gold
And the sheen of their spears were like stars on the sea
When the blue wave rolls nightly on deep Galilee

We had amended Byron's *Hebrew Melodies* a bit. We had changed 'The Assyrian' to 'The Afghan' and, perhaps, those Pathans did not clothe themselves in purple and gold and, naturally, the 'Galilee' bit is quite inappropriate. But the rhythm of the meter matched the jouncing of our car as it wove through the scrub-lands, driving into history. There, ahead of us, Afghans had created a magnificent fortified city on a 633 metre high plateau, 600 years ago.

The village of Mandu has grown inside the old fort.

Scrub lands gave way to rock-strewn, sub-montane slopes. Rising organically out of the bush and boulders, crumbling sentry-posts and watch-towers sped into view. The rugged topography could have influenced the Turkish Tughlaks to appoint the Afghani Ghoris to rule this territory as their governors. The Ghoris settled into their job only too well. Governor Dilawar Khan Ghori, sensing the declining powers of his overlords, declared himself independent of distant Delhi. His son, Alp Khan, went even further. When he ascended the throne in 1405, he changed his name to Hoshang Shah and shifted his capital to Mandu.

The great era of the plateau fortress had begun. The fortifications, in fact, are restricted to the perimeter of this vast complex. These frowning stone walls, however, formed only the second line of defence. As mountain men, the Afghans knew how to use topography to their advantage. Winding around the walls, and enclosing them, is the deep ravine of the Kakra Khoh. The walls hug the edge of the ravine and stretch around the plateau for about 45 kms. They are pierced by 12 formidable gates and we stopped at an oddly named one: The *Bhangi* gate. On a stone platform, just outside the gate, a few flowers had been carefully arranged around a small stick of incense sending a wavering blue plume into the still air. It told a cruel story. Here, when the gate was being built, the Afghans had sacrificed a low-caste man so that his soul would protect the gate. His name has been forgotten but someone still reveres his memory, six centuries later even though the Ghori dynasty had given way to their relatives, the Khiljis, then to the Mughals and the British and Mandu had finally become part of independent India.

We drove through the gate and into the fortress of Mandu. Unlike most of the austere and very aloof forts of Europe, frowning down on their villages, many of the forts of India embraced their civic societies. Fields and orchards, lakes, farms, livestock, artisans and traders all existed within the perimeter of the fort. Such forts were self-contained units able to survive the longest sieges because they drew their sustenance from within their walls. Mandu was such a fortress city though now, with the passing of the dynasties and their garrisons, it has subsided into a quiet hamlet.

That could well have been in a well-preserved caravanserai.

Its high, stone, walls enclosed a large court with a fountain in the centre and inward-facing rooms all around. Built into the massive walls of the single gate were sentry posts. Though all this was meant to serve caravans of traders and their pack animals, and goods, it could also have doubled as a slave market: a place where prospective buyers came to assess the quality of the 'goods' on offer. The high walls, narrow windows and guarded gate would ensure the security of this human merchandise before they were sold to their new owners. Then, when the fortunes of the fortress city declined and it became a hamlet, there were no slaves and no owners. Nevertheless, the green hamlet lives on, gentling the character of this old fortress-city.

The flower-bedecked grave at the Bhangi Gate.

Driving through Mandu, however, we soon realised that though it had been built as a fort it had evolved into a very exclusive pleasure resort. Inside these frowning battlements, Mandu soon became a place where Ghiyath-ud-Din, the ruler, had a seraglio of 15,000 women, a bodyguard of 500 beautiful Turkish females and an equal number of exquisite Abyssinian damsels. An ordinary man would have been pre-occupied with his in-house obligations, but Ghiyath-ud-Din was, clearly, made of sterner stuff. He found time to build the unique Hindola Mahal: the Swing Palace. It got its name from the fact that its massive, arched, walls slope inwards like the supports of a gigantic swing. It was, probably, an audience hall with fretted stone screens

We drove down its winding roads, past the bizarre-looking baobab trees grown from seeds brought in by trudging lines of African slaves. Local legend has it that they had chewed these seeds to quench their thirst on their trudge to the slave markets of Mandu.

which are works of art. Standing in the cool, striated shadows of the great hall, our minds filled it with the king holding court, surrounded by his glittering amazons: a powerful potentate in every sense of the term!

Later, his successors, the Mughal emperors, also used the pleasure domes of Mandu to unwind with their wives, concubines and courtiers.

We strolled down the main road of Mandu and to the stone stairs of the Jahaz Mahal: the so-called Ship Palace. It's a massive, sprawling, structure with squat towers, arches, pavilions and terraces. It thrusts out into a lake and, apparently, was meant to resemble a ship sailing. Clearly, the Afghans were not seamen! Nevertheless, the Jahaz Mahal still manages to capture an air of festivity in a rather traditional, heavy-handed, sort of way: as if the all-powerful ruler had issued a decree: 'Be Happy!' After which, everyone had celebrated with ordered pomp and dignity. Today, water-courses still curl with stylised formality, cupolas rise like the conical crowns of turbans, and where the tinkling laughter of women once filled the corridors, *mynahs* trill before they fly. The Mughal Emperor Jahangir was enchanted with the Jahaz Mahal and spent a blissful holiday here, besotted with the love of his life, the beautiful and intriguing Nur Jehan.

The Afghans thought that the Jahaz Mahal resembled a ship.

Both the Jahaz Mahal and the Hindola Mahal were festive places created by the sybaritic Ghiyath-ud-Din. His father, Hoshang Shah, clearly took a more serious view of life; and of death. His tomb, some way down the road from the Jahaz Mahal, is a sombre, hulking, structure with massive, fortress-like walls and crowned with a heavy dome. It radiates implacable power but very little grace as if its occupant had no time for such frivolities. In fact our guide asked us to enter with our shoes. This, apparently, was the emperor's expressed wish to indicate how little he thought of his own worldly majesty and glory! Such alleged humility seems a little odd because his was the first Indo-Islamic tomb to be made of white marble: a material once frowned upon for being too ostentatious! His daring innovation seems to have impressed his peers. Another legend has it that one

Above: Hindola Mahal's walls are shaped like the trustles of a swing. Right: The tomb of Hoshang Shah.

of the principal architects of the Taj Mahal had come to this tomb to seek inspiration for the design of that immortal memorial to love. But though his visit has, apparently, been recorded on the right jamb of the door to this tomb, the good Ustad Ahmed chose more graceful curves for that very feminine marble mausoleum in Agra.

Hoshang Shah's most majestic monument, however, rises deeper in the hamlet: the impressive Jami Masjid. The emperor did not live to see it completed but even in its present form, it is powerful. Covering an area of 97.4 sq m it has unique acoustic properties. The voice of even the most decrepit mullah can be heard, clearly, even at the far corners of the colonnaded prayer hall. This has, probably, been achieved by the many small domes on top of the hall and it might provide a fruitful research subject for an acoustic engineer.

For the best view of the mosque, we clambered up the steps of the Ashrafi Mahal, rising across the road from the mosque. It was started as a school by another great ruler of Mandu, Mahmud Khilji. Then he decided to raise it to a seven-storey tower to commemorate his victory over the Rana of Mewar in Rajasthan. The revised project, however, ran short of funds. Curiously, the Rana also celebrated his victory in that battle: he decided to raise his famous Tower of Victory in Chittor and, happily, was able to complete it.

The pulpit of the Jami Masjid.

The so-called pavilion of Rupamati was an observation point.

We followed a long line of tourists and visited the Palace of Baz Bahadur and the pavilion of his beloved, Rupamati. The Palace of this self-proclaimed ruler is an interesting multi-storeyed mansion built around a jade-green tank. A local guide waxed eloquent about Baz Bahadur's love for his shepherdess with a beautiful voice. He also wanted us to believe that the pavilion was built for her to glimpse her beloved plains. In fact the so-called Rupamati's Pavilion was really a look-out post for vigilant sentries. As for Baz Bahadur: when the Mughals invaded his territories in 1561, the timid king fled leaving Rupamati behind. The honourable Mughal General, Adham Khan, treated the captured Rupamati with great respect but she committed suicide. She must have been heart-broken when she realised that her Baz the Brave was no *bahadur*!

An avenue of baobabs grown from seeds carried by African slaves.

Finally, after paying courtesy calls to other monuments and listening to the many tales that generations of local people have woven around them, we drove to the Nilakantha Palace. This is a temple dedicated to Lord Shiva, now, but it had, probably, been built as a getaway by a powerful official of the fortress-city. We trudged down a long flight of stone steps to enter a roofless court enclosed by an open-fronted mansion. In the court was a tiled tank fed by a chaddar-cascade, all around were the high arches of apartments designed by someone who had a very modern appreciation of free-flowing spaces, light and air. It was perched at the edge of the escarpment and one side of the court was open to the wooded valley falling away below. For a hard-working high official, it must have offered a cool, serene, green escape all through the year.

The name of this aesthetic official was probably Shirwan Shah and, clearly, he had no illusions about his future. A verse inscribed in this sylvan retreat, as rendered by us, reads:

In the balcony of Shirwan Shah
A dawn owl hooted a warning
Revel in your pomp and glory now
It will flee as the night pales to morning.

This could well have been the epitaph of Mandu.

The Jewel in the Lotus

UJJAIN

Here, quite literally, time is of the essence.

We wound our way through queue lines, metal detectors, frisking and into the grounds of the great temple of Mahakaleshwar: The Lord of Time. Beyond and around the temple tank lesser temples rose but we stepped through a silver door of the towering main temple and trod down a flight of steps. In the centre of the sanctum rose the black Shivling worshipped as Mahakaleshwar. A priest accepted the offerings of worshippers, chanted his invocations in a low voice; the worshippers moved on, more pilgrims took their place. It was a ceaseless acknowledgement of the most implacable force in the universe. In that small chamber, heavy with the fragrance of flowers, incense and devotion it struck us that no other religion had deified so all-pervasive a reality as Time.

That is what had drawn us back to Ujjain. We wanted to explore, once again, this ancient city's mélange of science and faith capturing the span of a unique religion.

Mahakaleshwar, one of the twelve Jyotirlingas.

When we emerged into the sunlight again, our guide said, "Perhaps Mahakaleshwar was worshipped by the Indus Valley people. Many believe that some Harappans settled here after fleeing from their stricken cities. It was they, those skilled seafarers, who established our Prime Meridian in our city." A Prime Meridian is the zero longitude from which all other longitudes take their position. The modern one stretches through the Royal Observatory

Astronomers in the Vedha Shala take readings on a traditional instrument.

in Greenwich, England. Our guide wasn't finished. "Our Prime Meridian was laid down in 1,800 BC, long before the Britishers." We nodded, not convinced about his Harappan theory. "You know," he added, "that the Tropic of Cancer passes through Ujjain. This is where winter changes to spring. So we established a great observatory here. It is indeed a wonderful place."

He directed us through the winding roads of this old city.

In the dusk, aarti lamps twinkle across the Shipra River.

The board outside read Vedha Shala. In the open grounds stood huge masonry structures that looked like enormous versions of a child's geometry set. At one end was a low, barrack-like building. Here we met two unassuming, soft-spoken, astronomer-mathematicians: Pandits Bharat Tiwari and Giriwar Prasad Sharma. They took us around and explained the purpose of some of the strange creations. One was an enormous sundial called the Samrat Yantra: it indicated solar time with the accuracy of a few seconds. Then there was a dramatic red wall with two white arcs crossing it. This was a Transit Instrument. There were also three other massive constructions but we couldn't quite fathom their purpose. All these were erected between 1725 and 1730 by Maharaja Jai Singh of Jaipur, governor of Ujjain. Jai Singh had built similar ones in Delhi and Jaipur, but this is the only one still being used as an observatory. With the help of these remarkable instruments, the pandits write an annual ephemeris giving the predicted positions of nine celestial bodies for a whole year. These meticulously accurate charts are widely circulated and referred to by astrologers all over India while preparing horoscopes governing the lives of crores of believers. Ujjain's is, undoubtedly, the most unusual and influential observatory in the world.

This is not the only place in Ujjain dedicated to the heavens. We walked to the banks of the softly-flowing Shipra River and up a few steps to a temple dedicated to the Navagrahas: the nine celestial bodies of astrology. The idols of the Sun, Moon, and their ascendant and descendant modes,

The Mahakaleshwar Temple, the heart of Ujjain.

Venus, Mercury, Mars, Jupiter and Saturn are just heads with indistinct features but they are held in great reverence. According to their devotees, their influences make or mar people's lives.

Still on Ujjain's celestial trail, we visited the Temple of Mangalnath. It rises at the top of a hillock with clear views all around and is, according to the pujari, the place where the planet Mars was born. There is an idol of him with his vahan, a ram. Obviously, human eyes were much sharper then than they are now; and at that time there was virtually no light pollution. Quite possibly, it was from this high place that local sky watchers identified the red planet for the first time, recording it as the birth of Mars.

This catholic acceptance of new ideas by the people of Ujjain, and their willingness to enshrine them as a part of their faith, is clear from the number of temples, their deities, and forms of worship, which enrich this town.

We climbed up the steps of the Harsiddhi Ma temple complex and stood next to two towering, cone-shaped, *deepstambhs*, or 'light pillars', built by the Marathas when they ruled Ujjain. This temple of the Mother Goddess stands on an elevated plinth and the idol enthroned here is Chandni in her aspect of Harsiddhi: The One Who Vanquishes All. Its ceiling holds the powerful Sri Yantra, prime emblem of the Mother. This complex geometric design is said to induce a heightened state of consciousness if meditated upon. When these mental Doors of Perception are opened the mind finds solutions to seemingly intractable problems in a way that apparently happens to shamans in their self-induced trances.

Or so our more spiritually inclined friends would have us believe.

In front of this temple is one of the estimated fifty-one Shakti Peeths in India, Pakistan, Bangladesh, Nepal, Tibet and Sri Lanka. The Shakti Peeths identify the places on which the dismembered body and jewellery of the consort of Lord Shiva fell. She had immolated herself because her spouse had been insulted by her father. Devotees cannot enter this sunken temple but may view the idol through the three peep-holes cut into its ceiling. There, below, an eternal flame burns to one side and, according to believers,

In the Harsiddhi Ma temple stands the red shrine to Shakti.

the fallen elbow of Sati has been enshrined. Along with these mysterious Shakti Peeths, the worship of the primal Mother Goddesses, also referred to as Matrikas, could have been mankind's first religion, associating the generative power of women with the creative powers of nature. This, eventually, led to the esoteric, female-centred, cult of Tantra. According to scholars, Ujjain was a centre of Tantric rituals in the past though Tantrism was forced underground as Vedic orthodoxy grew in the north and west of our land.

Leaving them behind we drove out through scrub and farm-land to the greatly revered Sandipani Ashram, claiming a very unusual origin. This small complex of buildings, set in a garden, is of particular interest to the devotees of Lord Krishna. Here, apparently, the sage Sandipani taught Lord Krishna, Balram and Sudama. The original ashram, we were told, has been rebuilt as a temple enshrining the idol of Sandipani. Facing their guru, and at a befittingly lower level, are images of his three star pupils including the only sitting idol of Krishna. The head priest here was Rupam Vyas who informed

The Ram Ghat just before aarti.

The Banyan tree called Siddhavat on the banks of the Shipra.

us that he was the 202nd direct descendant of the guru. The shivling in the shrine in front of the Sandipani Temple represents Harihara, a composite of Vishnu and Shiva. The worshippers of Vishnu and Shiva were often at loggerheads. The combined image of the two gods sought to bring the two cults together. A pujari here also explained that as the Vishnu aspect of Harihara incorporates his incarnation Krishna, the Nandi in front of this idol stands, and does not sit as he is usually depicted, in honour of the cowherd prince. We found this richly complex explanation fascinating. It is believed that the tank in the ashram was created by Lord Krishna who caused the River Gomti to bubble up here so that his guru, who was from Mathura, could bathe in its sacred waters. Krishna also washed his slate in this tank and so it is known as both Gomti Kund and Ankpat.

Then we went to a shrine which claimed even greater antiquity.

We parked our car and walked to the edge of a terrace rising from the banks of the Shipra River. Here stood the reputedly immortal Siddhavat Tree. It was said to have been planted by Sita and its roots go down to the nether world. This is why devotees come here to share in rituals for the repose of the souls of their relatives. Families sat around officiating priests, in small groups, and performed their memorial ceremonies. The Siddhavat is also a *kalpavriksh*, a wish-fulfilling tree. Pilgrims tied threads to it in a custom that webs the world: we've seen it being done at the shrine of the Mother of Christ in Turkey's Ephesus. Here, however, milk is also poured on its branches and coconuts offered in a very Indic variation. Seeing us taking photographs, a bystander with a professorial beard and a very scholarly manner, intoned, "The scene that you see here, today, is as old as the Vedas."

He was probably right and we felt we were experiencing rituals dating back to the time when the Vedic people had settled in the Indo-Gangetic plain and had begun to absorb pre-Vedic deities into their fold.

We drove through more truly rural terrain and parked outside the walled grounds of the Godkalika Mandir. A descriptive board at the entrance of the complex said that the great poet Kalidas had worshipped here and that the temple showed evidence of repairs and renovations from the first century BC to the modern reign of the Scindias. The single-celled temple sits on a plinth in the centre of a small courtyard with rooms all around. The idol of Kalika is a red head wearing a silver crown. It is simple, unsophisticated and, clearly, represents a primal deity possibly worshipped by early tribal communities. An interesting legend says that Kalidas' genius blossomed only after he had prayed to Kalika which is why many of the important verses in his famed poem, *Meghadootham*, describe the glories of Ujjain.

Another, possibly tribal, deity worshipped as an idol which was just a red head, was Kalbhairav. In his full form he is a hunter accompanied by a black dog. There were dogs in the grounds of his walled temple crowning a lightly wooded knoll. Outside the temple, stalls sold small bottles of liquor because alcohol is one of the gifts accepted by this deity. It is poured into a plate and then tippled into the lips of the idol. Devotees believe that the spirituous offering is consumed miraculously.

Kalbhairav was originally considered to be one of the warriors of Lord Shiva but now many people accept him as an aspect of his Lord. This has also occurred to Ganesh. Neither he nor his father Shiva are mentioned in the Vedas but, later, after Shiva becomes one of the trinity, Ganesh also acquired the title Ganapati: the leader of Lord Shiva's hosts.

We visited two temples dedicated to Lord Ganesh. One holds a huge, man-made idol of the elephant-headed god, now recognised as the God of Good Beginnings. The other is a fairly small idol in the subterranean chamber of a temple accessed through a ground level foyer with excellently carved pillars. The idol of the Chintamani Ganesh who removes worries, is a natural formation as are those of the flanking idols regarded as his wives Riddhi and Siddhi. Clearly, these were worshipped long before the temple was built over them.

The first temples were not built-up structures but caves with their interiors often sculpted and carved. Some distance out of Ujjain, a long flight of steps led down from the road to a terrace on the banks of the Shipra River. There we saw a sadhu sitting under the shade of a tree, reading. Behind him was a low, white, building with a single door set in it. We went in and entered a courtyard. To the left was a shrine and steps led up two interlinked caves. An information board identified these as the Bhartrihari Caves and said that they were all that remained of a double-storeyed monastery of the Nath sect. There was an interesting carving showing a two-armed dancing

Shiva carrying maces but the other images in the caves seemed to be modern additions installed to attract pilgrims. A young ascetic and a much older one sat in front of two of the idols ready to minister to visitors.

We were disappointed in the caves but the fact that they had once been a centre of the Nath cult interested us. The Naths, who can be identified by a metal ring pierced through one of their ears, are an unusual group. They worship Lord Shiva but they call their spiritual leaders '*Pirs*', titles usually conferred on Muslim saints. Some distance away from the caves, and standing by itself surrounded by fields, was the very Islamic looking mausoleum of the Nath Pir Matsyendranath. It was covered by a chaddar in the Muslim manner, but this sheet wasn't green, but saffron. The tombs of the Nath Pirs, we were told by our guide, are revered by both Hindus and Muslims. Our rare *Encyclopaedia Asiatica* written by the very learned Edward Balfour says: 'Nath is the term more especially employed by a particular sect, that of the Yogi or Pasupata, the oldest sect probably existing now amongst the Hindus.'

These brotherhoods of ascetics are grouped into self-governing orders called *akharas* under a mahant. They are often regarded with considerable awe because of their reputed magical powers and awesome appearance. Years ago we witnessed the ritual bathing of the Naga sect of sadhus in the famed Kumbh Mela here, in Ujjain. This happens once in twelve years to commemorate another celestial event: the legendary spilling of the nectar produced by the churning of the ocean. An immersion in the river at the auspicious moment absolves one of all sin, but the Naga sadhus demand, and get, precedence over others.

That was an unforgettable encounter. We had driven out in the cold of pre-dawn and taken our seats under an awning set up on the banks of the sacred river. A chill breeze brought the sound of distant drums and the murmur of a great crowd approaching. Then we saw them. The columns of naked, ash-smeared, Nagas with coiled and bleached locks,

Gateway to the temple of the famous hunter Kalbhairav.

strode determinedly, carrying their mahant in an open palanquin like the powerful potentate that he was to them. Drummers thudding lustily, preceded him, khaki-clad policemen held back inquisitive crowds. Masses of devotees streamed behind. The Nagas lined up on the banks of the Shipra with their portly mahant standing in their midst like a great, venerated, grey idol. The drumming stopped. There was a trembling air of anticipation. The first rays of the sun touched the flowing river, burnishing it like molten metal. With a full-throated roar, the Nagas plunged in, immersing themselves in a splashing, churning, catharsis of absolution. The river turned quicksilver with the ash off their bodies. And only when this eldritch host of Shiva had emerged, dripping and glistening, from their bath, did the lay pilgrims dare to immerse themselves in a teeming, classless, celebration of mass bathing at the sacred *kumbh*.

Like the faithful, we had immersed ourselves in the brimming religious heritage of Ujjain, but we had one more encounter left.

As sunset approached, we drove across a bridge spanning the Shipra River and went to the west bank ghats below the Monastery of Dutta Akhada. Ram Ghat, rising out of the far bank, shimmered atop its reflections as if they had been embossed on watered silk. A small percussion band and a devotee with a conch gathered near us. And then, at sunset, just as the lights winked on like fireflies all over Ujjain, a lone young pujari on our side began the evocative fire ritual of *aarti*. The oil lamp he held aloft encircled him in a garland of golden fire as he swayed, raised it and moved it in graceful worship. From the Ram Ghat opposite, a number of bare-chested pujaris replicated his movements setting the dark river aflame with their shifting reflections. The drums beat, the cymbals crashed, the conch called, the moving lights spun swift, luminous, webs in the water capturing our minds in a spell that bridged countless centuries.

And it gave us our own moment of truth. Hinduism has evolved out of an ocean of beliefs, rituals and practices. Its roots spread deep in the rich sludge and ooze at the bottom, but the lotus flower rises above it all, floating unsullied on the surface. In the heart of the flower lies a jewel each of whose facets reflects a unique and very personal approach to reality. The options for seekers are unlimited.

This is the real, esoteric, meaning of the mantra: Hail to the Jewel in the Lotus.

The First Gallery

BHIMBETKA

In Madhya Pradesh we entered a Time Machine.

We looked at a world as it was 35,000 years ago. Herds of elephant, rhinoceros and enormous bison had haunted the great moist forests which had covered much of this land. Here, men armed with puny weapons had to defend themselves and then to hunt these animals for food. It was an uncertain life and they sought out high, rocky, places from where they could spot approaching danger. They chose rock-shelters because caves had limited exits and overhanging shelves of rock offered more opportunities to spot, and escape from, predators. To increase their chances of survival, however, they evoked the magic of imagery. If they could capture the spirit of those who threatened them then, perhaps, they could control them. And so they began to paint their fears and hopes on the walls of their shelters creating an enchantment that still ensnares us.

A hunter rides a prehistoric elephant.

In quest of this ancient vision, we drove out of Bhopal, heading towards the hill station of Pachmarhi. After 45 kms we turned, bumped over a level crossing, and ascended a boulder-strewn hillock where *palas* flowers bloomed as livid as clotted blood. Below us, eroded plains spread resembling the terrain in the Olduvai Gorge in Tanzania. There the Leakeys had made their discoveries about early man. It did seem to us that our Stone Age ancestors, world-wide, preferred a certain type of topography for their settlements. The one ahead of us, now, in Bhimbetka, certainly had many defensive advantages.

At the end of the stone-flagged path a huge outcrop of rocks towered like a great and forbidding bastion. At the start of the path, the Archaeological Survey of India had erected a board giving information about what lay ahead. Among other things, it said:

These caves were discovered in 1957-58. Out of the 750 rock shelters, 500 are adorned with paintings. This was the centre of human activity right from Lower Palaeolithic times up to the Medieval period. The cup marks made on the rocks date back to 100,000 BP. This pushed back the date of the cognitive development of man at Bhimbetka to many thousand years earlier than similar sites in various parts of the world making it the earliest cognitive human evolution.

'BP' is Before the Present. The term 'cognitive human evolution' must be the ASI's way of identifying the emergence of humans from our hominid, ape-like, ancestors. Most surprising, however, is the claim that humans lived in these shelters one hundred thousand years ago. According to scientists involved in the Human Genome Diversity Project, humans began to migrate out of Africa only fifty to sixty thousand years ago. In other words, the people who made the cup marks on the rock shelters ahead, had evolved in India, which makes them unique. We, however, felt that this question should be answered by the experts. We strode ahead, up the path through the trees leading to the great outcrop of rock hiding the wonders of Bhimbetka. At the end of the path we climbed a short flight of stone steps and stood in front of a high, open-ended, cave.

As a very rough and ready rule of thumb, the oldest paintings are green or dark red. Their lines are simple and no humans appear. Interestingly, the earliest paintings show no conflicts between warring tribes. Clearly, the world was not a crowded place then and so there was no need to kill our fellow creatures to acquire their territories! Also, the most recent paintings are, often, the crudest as if the very process of building a material civilisation had destroyed the artists' power to tap the intuitive abilities so necessary for all great works of art. Horses appear in the middle period because they were, possibly, introduced into our land by the nomadic Indo-Iranian steppe people, later referred to as the Aryans. But all these are technical considerations which, in a way, detract

Entrance to the Stone Age rock shelters of Bhimbetka.

A racing rider and a rearing horse.

from the empathic enjoyment of Bhimbetka. Our greatest discovery, in fact, came quite by accident.

We had just rounded a massive rise of rock when the sun lanced down through the *sal* trees, straight into our eyes. Instinctively, we raised our heads to deflect the beam, and we glimpsed it. Something shone red on a rock high above us. We stepped right, left, forward, backward. It blurred, vanished, glistened again. And only from one place did it leap out clearly. A huge red bison had been caught, charging, head lowered, at a desperately fleeing man. The bison was enormous, blown out of proportion by the stark terror of the man, running for his life. Somehow, we feel he never made it. But the agony of his last, frightened, seconds was frozen, down untold centuries, on this rock.

After this our 'discoveries' came fast and thick.

On a plum-coloured slab, two bull elephants with huge tusks stood out. One had two hunters on its back, spearing it to death. Elephants were common in Bhimbetka in those, moist, lush days. Another intriguing picture had been painted on a pale cliff, fissured by the questing roots of trees. There were horned deer, here, probably sambar, but two of them had loops on their backs which looked like saddles. In fact there was a chair-like structure above these animals which could well have been a primitive saddle. If this vignette does depict saddled deer then we've made quite a discovery. Today, the only deer used as pack and riding animals are reindeer domesticated by the Sami of Finland. This prehistoric painting could, therefore, prove that the art of domesticating deer existed and was lost in India in the distant past. But there was something even more interesting here. When we looked carefully to the left of this scene, we saw someone's right hand with an amputated index finger. The line of amputation has been clearly shown as has the upper bit of the finger that was removed. We know that early humans did operations but this is the first time that anyone has noticed such a surgical feat in Bhimbetka.

And then, on another overhang, there was a vivid hunting scene. Men fired arrows at animals, hurled throwing sticks, protected themselves with large shields, and were psyched to greater efforts by a larger-than-life shaman in a horned headdress. The presence of the shaman gave us reason to believe that most of these paintings were manifestations of sympathetic magic. If images of hunters were depicted slaughtering paintings of animals then, possibly, living hunters would be able to kill real animals. This association of rock-paintings with magic has been commented on by the *Encyclopaedia Britannica*. Referring to the almost total absence of human figures in the earliest cave art, it says:

> Such human figures as do appear in (early) cave art are almost always disguised in some way, either combined with animal forms, or crudely drawn with distorted, mask like faces. Possibly the enormous power of art made men reluctant to subject themselves to its control.

A terrifyingly huge bison chasing a fleeing man.

Stampeding animals in the 'zoo' shelter.

We were reminded of one of our trips into the higher, and more remote, Himalayas. Here a tribe of people refused, quite aggressively, to let us photograph them: "No! No!" they shouted. "When you take our photographs you imprison parts of our souls!"

Consequently, a gifted painter, in those distant days, could well have been as revered as a seer, spared of other duties so that he could work his magic for the good of the tribe. And so, mixing coloured earths, vegetable dyes, soot and animal fat, the Stone Age artist applied them with brushes shredded out of fibrous twigs or filled charcoal outlines with fat and then blew on powders through hollow bones. The latter technique created subtly tinted pictures with the delicate, three-dimensional, finish of Japanese brush-work. And while he did this, the sounds of the chants and spells around him convinced the artist that his evocative painting would never fade. And, in a way, he was right. In course of time, the natural pigments became absorbed by the cellular structure of the rocks, and slowly, they became as permanent as tattoos on human skin.

Which is why we, who live today, can still view that magical world through eyes that are many millennia old. We can still travel in the time machine that is Bhimbetka.

Bundela Towers and Intrigues

ORCHHA

It is a medieval romance.

Orchha has all the dark and glittering qualities of a tale sung by troubadours on the rush-spread floors of heraldic castles. There's murder and treachery, noble kings and beautiful courtesans and the writhing convolutions of royal intrigues. Woven through it all is sybaritic indulgence,

A venerable singing sadhu.

a secret cellar cooled by sky-high winds and an idol that doggedly refused to move from its chosen abode. All this in a town where an itinerant scent-seller still peddles his vials of ittar and custard apples hang luscious against the massive stone walls of a river-encircled fortress.

We like fairy tales and fantasies and when there are veins of truth running through them, we like them even better.

Sixteen kilometres from Jhansi, our road wound through the eroded, rugged, scrub-lands of Madhya Pradesh. The Betwa, that legendary river, chuckled to herself, then snarled as black rocks dared to impede her progress. On a hillock, gazing down at the moating river, were watch towers crenellated forts and regal palaces. Rising in other prominent places were temples and cenotaphs with pinnacles like knobbly pinecones. In the flatlands between the fortress, palaces and temples, a hamlet grew and spread and continues to live. Here there are narrow streets where the tiled roofs and the turquoise coloured facades of the cottages hide cool, secluded, courtyards. Life in the hamlet has changed little since the days when the Bundela rajas built their palaces in the 16th century.

They wanted to tell the Great Mughal in Delhi that they, too, were a power to be reckoned with. Not quite defiant but not to be taken for granted.

We drove through one of the great gates of the citadel, across an arched stone bridge spanning a curve of the Betwa and climbed a rising fortress road. To our left was the mass of the fortress-palace: the old Raj Mahal with its angled light shafts to deter Peeping Toms and its sensuous frescoes. To our right was the Jehangir Mahal, screened from the public eye by the palace and architecturally more appealing than the Raj Mahal. Prince Madhukar Shah, a scion of the old Bundela dynasty, informed us that:

Lutyens, the architect of New Delhi, used this palace as his inspiration for his New Delhi buildings.

In front of us, like a bridge between the two, was the sybaritic addition of the luxury

The 'pinecone' cenotaphs of the Bundelas.

suite, and the terraces and domes of the Sheesh Mahal. Here, high above the hamlet, fort and palace was a secluded haven for royal pleasure. Before its renovation, its ceiling had inset mirrors and a further set of cheval mirrors gave uninterrupted views of the bathroom from the king-sized bed.

Clearly the Bundelas had very regal tastes, greatly influenced by their Mughal overlords. Both the Raj and Jehangir Mahals were built in their assertive style featuring labyrinths of corridors, halls, living quarters, terraces and high cupolas. Legend has it that the Jehangir Mahal was built for the patron of Bir Singh, the Mughal Emperor Jehangir.

The grisly story goes that Salim hated the wise old Afzal Khan, the far-seeing advisor to his father, Emperor Akbar. He wanted to have Afzal Khan beheaded and the grey-beard's head brought to him on a platter. The Bundela Prince, Bir Singh, longed to take over the throne of Orchha from his gentle brother Ram Shah, and was willing to do anything to get his way. He had his goons assassinate the old man, decapitated him, and presented Afzal Khan's head to Salim exactly as he'd wanted to see it: on a platter, gory and bleeding!

When Salim became the Emperor Jehangir on the death of his father, he rewarded the unscrupulous Bir Singh, gave him the throne of Orchha and moved Ram Shah to the neighbouring state of Chanderi. But for all his skulduggery, Bir Singh proved to be a creative king. He built the massive

Intricate murals embellish Orchha's old palaces.

The palace of the brilliant courtesan, Rai Praveen.

Jehangir Mahal for his emperor and even, possibly, constructed a mosque for his patron. History does not say if Jehangir ever visited Orchha or if the mosque was ever used by the followers of the Prophet.

We walked around the citadel, admired the frescoes in its royal chambers; saw the strategically placed mirrors in the pleasure apartment on the terrace, the Sheesh Mahal; visited the high-roofed stables that once...we were assured... held camels and elephants; admired the sybaritic bath house, the Hamam...hot baths, steam rooms, chill pools, massage tables, a medieval spa for all reasons; and delighted in the garden mansion of the talented courtesan, Rai Praveen.

She was the mistress of one of the rulers but tales of her beauty and wit had spread so far that her royal lover received an imperial summons directing her to join the harem of the Mughal Emperor. The penalty for disobeying such a command was death, so she left Orchha in a royal caravan and was carried to the Mughal court. But she also took, with her, a poem that she had written for her powerful admirer. Our translation is:

Dogs and crows and the scavenging crew
Dine on the leavings of others.
Tell me my Emperor, and tell me true,
Which of these three pariahs are you?

She returned in triumph to Orchha and the arms of her princely lover.

Driving down from the citadel, across the stone bridge, we visited the impressive Chatturbhuj Temple. It is dedicated to the four-armed Lord Vishnu but it has many of the aspects of a mosque and could, originally, have been built by Bir Singh for his imperial patron. Among other significant peculiarities in the temple, the experts of the Delhi School of Architecture and Planning point out that:

> The absence of any carving or ornamentation, the loftiness of the ceilings, and the arrangement of its sanctuary are unusual features in a Hindu temple.

We clambered down the steps of the platform of the temple, wound our way along a street teeming with colourful hawkers, past a line of mendicants, and entered the Ram Raja Temple. This looks very much like the palace it once was. In the 18th century, the principal queen of the ruler, Madhukar Shah, brought back an image of Lord Rama with the intention of installing it in its own temple. But after she set it down in a place of honour in her palace, the idol could not be shifted. And so the Queen's palace became a temple. Inside the sanctum of this Palace-turned-temple, the idol of Lord Rama was dressed as a Maharaja crowned with a large, regal, turban. To his left was Sita, wearing a crown, and to his right was Lakshmana, also wearing a turban. According to a local legend, from the day that the idol of Lord Rama was installed here, Madhukar Shah refused to spend a night in Orchha because he felt that there wasn't any room in the town for two rajas!

The gentle Madhukar Shah made the interesting Phool Bagh near the Ram Raja Temple. This was not just a garden but an arched, pillared and domed water-cooled summer palace. Aqueducts ran on top of its walled garden, fed fountains cascading down from the ceiling of a pavilion to simulate monsoon rain, and then filled a cistern shaped like a wine cup before flowing into a scalloped pool. The huge basements of the Phool Bagh were also cooled by two high towers. Wind blowing across the top of these enormous chimneys apparently used the Venturi Effect to suck air out of the large cellars and draw in a cool draught from the Phool Bagh. These two naturally air-conditioning towers were known as *Dastgirs* and are the only examples of these Persian structures. No one knows who brought this concept to Orchha.

We walked across to the very simple monument called the Hardaul ka Baithak. Raja Jujhar Singh's noble half-brother held court in this double-storeyed Rajasthani mansion. Legend has it that he would address his large number of admirers from a pavilion in his garden, now known as his seat. The story connected with this place is a typically convoluted medieval intrigue. According to our guide, the Mughals suspected that Hardaul was using his popularity to raise an army to challenge them. They convinced

The wind tapping towers from Iran.

the ruler, Jujhar Singh, that his wife was having an affair with Hardaul. His wife was shocked when Jujhar accused her of this. She reminded him that when Hardaul's mother had died, she had brought up the boy as her own son. But Jujhar, blinded by jealously, gave her an ultimatum. Unless she poisoned Hardaul, he would not believe her. Anguished, she carried the fatal meal to Hardaul but when she put it before him, he asked her why she had tears in her eyes. She blurted out the truth and begged him not to eat it. But Hardaul said, "If I don't eat this food then there'll be distrust between husbands and wives all over the kingdom." Hardaul's seat is now a shrine where his idol is worshipped and, to this day, the first wedding invitation distributed by any family in this area is laid in Hardaul's pavilion.

We left the sad tale of Hardaul and drove up to an unusual building with happier associations. The Laxminarayan Temple is a square structure with a central court holding a shrine. Its entrance is in one of its diagonals. The outer walls of the building are bare but the inner walls are profusely painted. There are scenes of war, the storming of the fort of Jhansi by British

Above: The temple where Rama is enthroned as a king.
Below: The unusual Laxminarayan Temple.

troops, and the depictions of an enormous mythological creature carrying elephants in its claws, a woman warrior mounted on a horse, hunting a tiger, two foreigners, in breeches and hats, drinking at a table with a happy dog at their feet. The scenes seemed to be far too martial and secular to have been suitable for a temple. This building had probably been designed as a royal gazebo, a summer pavilion cooled by winds and giving uninterrupted views of the river valley and converted into a temple later.

Our guide, S.P. Misra of the State's Archaeological Department, explained how many of these red-and-white pictures had been created. According to him, sea shells were ground into a powder and then made into a paste which was plastered on panels on the walls. This was then polished till it has the sheen of marble. This was painted over with a red coat made from an extract of *palas* flowers. Finally, the pattern was scratched onto the red surface so that the white under-surface appeared. In Switzerland, where we first noticed such decorations, we learnt that the technique is called *sgraffito,* an Italian word dating back to the 1730s. Misra informed us that the *sgraffito* in Orchha were from the 19th century. We wondered if the two partying foreigners with their happy dog had had anything to do with it.

A little before sunset we got into an inflatable raft for a short jouncing, bouncing, swirling, twirling, spinning, spraying encounter with the Betwa when she foams with anger at the rocks that stand in her path. The

In the Laxminarayan Temple, a woman warrior dominates a graffiti-scarred painting.

river-rafting here is in the skilled hands of the MP Tourism Development Corporation's boatmen. One of us does not swim and yet we would like to do this bucketing ride over and over again. This river run also gave us an excellent view of the fifteen, cone-shaped, cenotaphs of the Bundela rulers. They looked beautifully eerie in the saffron light of the low sun with the ominous silhouettes of large vultures flying around them like vampires from some gothic horror story. But it did place Orchha in an appropriately Middle Ages setting. And so, when we were bobbing past the tombs we thought of the tale that the present prince Madhukar Shah, had told us.

Sometimes, at night, he wrote, people have seen a ghostly rider *clip-clopping* down the medieval streets of Orchha.

Above: A mythical chungi chiriya *in the Laxminarayan Temple. Left: River rafting on the Betwa.*

There Be Whyte Tygres

BANDHAVGARH

In November we escaped into sanity.

Though our cottage sits in its own wood in the Himalayas, it's a very small wood. So, every once in a while, we have to abandon schedules, mobile phones, computers and our saw-edged, harrowing 21st century world. We flee from our wired cottage in our oak wood into a wider, wilder, wilderness. There, we breathe in vast green spaces, recharge our jaded psyches. The most recharging jungles are those where tigers roam free.

In winter we chose the Bandhavgarh Tiger Reserve in the Vindhya Ranges of Madhya Pradesh.

White tigers were first found in Bandhavgarh.

In an area of 1,580 sq kms, Bandhavgarh has between 47 to 71 tigers, according to Dr. Yadavendradev Jhala of the Wildlife Institute, Dehra Dun. As the tiger has a wide range, there is always a fair chance of spotting one of these magnificent animals in this reserve. Bandhavgarh has two other unique qualifications. It's where the white tigers were first introduced into captivity; and it was the home of a very famous tiger, the formidable Charger.

We had seen him in action the last time we had visited Bandhavgarh. Driving out on a morning round, with guide Jagat Narayan Chaturvedi, we had crossed another jeep when its driver called out. He said that a tiger had been spotted and elephants had been stationed to view the great cat. We bumped through the jungle roads, stopped, mounted the small 'two-seater' elephant which had been allotted to us, and lumbered through the trees and scrub. Ahead of us, other elephants, with other tourists, had encircled a fairly large area. Here, bamboos had grown into bushy clumps about two to three metres high. The tiger had made a chital kill, dragged it into the bamboo thickets, and was lying in a small clearing in the heart of the thickets.

We had to shift and manoeuvre to get shots of the resting tiger because the bamboos came in the way. We would have gone closer but we knew that animals have well-established comfort zones. If strangers step into these zones, they could be attacked. Our guide had told us to be particularly careful of this animal because he was the alpha male, the acknowledged boss, of the range, and his name was Charger.

Mounting an elephant from a jeep.

A tiger and his kill.

We soon found out how he had got that name.

Two young English women sitting on another elephant, were, obviously, not aware of Charger's reputation. They urged their *mahawat*...elephant drivers are called *mahawats* here, mahouts in some other forests...to take them closer. Unwisely he did.

Charger sat up: his comfort zone breached. His furious roar reverberated through the forest. He bounded forward, and leapt.

The women screamed and drew up their bare legs. If Charger had really intended to attack he would have dragged one of them down and mauled her. But he had not felt threatened, only insulted, so they escaped unscathed. Charger returned to the shelter of his thicket, growling his warning softly.

It had been such a sudden attack that not one of the many cameras had recorded it.

Sadly, that was the last time we saw Charger. Forest officials believe that he had a terrible fight with his eldest son, was dethroned, and died shortly afterwards. But as he had fathered many cubs with his mate, Sita, his striped genes still prowl the jungles of Bandhavgarh. We hoped to meet some of his progeny on this trip.

We were staying in the White Tiger Forest Lodge, in a stilt cottage raised above the forest floor. We had arrived in the late forenoon, had lunch, and were getting ready for the afternoon round when a thud hit our roof, followed by agonised squeals. We rushed out onto the catwalk that linked the rooms.

When you live at the edge of a jungle, thuds on the roof are alarming. To our surprise, the ominous sounds had been made by a tribe of monkeys, leaping from roof to roof. Most unusually, for these socially bonded animals, they were attacking a female of their family. Later, the staff informed us that the male monkeys were punishing a cowering female for dropping her baby from the roof, carelessly. This showed such a highly developed sense of social accountability that we were reluctant to believe them. But all those of the staff who were local people assured us that this was true and that such behaviour had often been observed in this tribe of langurs.

If their assumptions were correct then it showed that the langurs had evolved societal responses to an almost human level. The lives of the males in the troupe had not been endangered by the negligent mother, but the survival of the group had. She was being admonished because she had jeopardised the future of the extended family. It was disturbingly near the judgments meted out to erring members by *khap panchayats* in our rural north.

This is one reason why we find our forests fascinating.

We believe that a natural forest, one that has been allowed to grow at its own pace over decades, becomes a living entity. Its trees and wildlife are as closely integrated as the organs, blood and cells in our bodies. Thus, rain falling on the mountains surrounding Bandhavgarh enriches the forests, meadows and wetlands of the Tiger Reserve. These in turn provide sustenance for wildlife: from the insects, birds and reptiles, to the herds of herbivores and, finally, at the top of the food chain, to the flesh-eating carnivores. And in their quest to find a niche in the forest's eco-system, wild

A spotted deer and a vigilant langur.

The wild landscape of Bandhavgarh.

creatures are inter-dependent on each other for survival and they evolve, as the langurs seem to have done.

Also, as in all living creatures, even in a symbiotic relationship, generations of survival in the forests does, occasionally, throw up a long-dormant recessive gene. It's much like a light-eyed baby being born into a dark-eyed family because, in the distant past, a blue-eyed ancestor had made his contribution to the family's genetic pool.

This happened to the tigers of Bandhavgarh. According to Dr. Jhala, tigers had first appeared in Central China. One stream had migrated north-westwards into the Caspian, the other had taken a southern route. As in the epic of human migration out of Africa, the bodies of succeeding generations had adapted to changing environments. The Siberian race had become larger, whiter, to survive in their harsh, snow-bound, land; the Indian strain had slimmed down and become the 18th century's

Tygre! Tygre! burning bright
In the forests of the night
What immortal hand or eye
Could frame thy fearful symmetry?

We couldn't resist the medieval spelling. But it was neither an immortal hand nor eye which gave the Indian tiger his black stripes. It was the need to merge into the striated shadows of our grasslands in which they now

hunted. But sometimes, the white gene surfaced. It had done so in these jungles, and the ruling family of Rewa had captured them and bred them to produce all the white tigers now known to the world. Today, there were no white tigers in the wild although the white gene must still survive, particularly among the wild tigers of Bandhavgarh and could reappear in a future family of tigers. Moreover, because tigers are being protected in our Reserves, all creatures large and small down the line are also sheltered

Above: A tiger resting in a bamboo thicket.
Below: A pair of timid Barking Deer.

under the tiger's umbrella. We saw wild pig and sambar and on the forested side of a *maidan* of white-plumed grass, we heard the alarm call of a chital. Then we saw the deer standing in a shaft of sunlight, its right hoof raised in fear. A langur barked in anxiety. The chital panicked and sped across the road. A tiger rippled through the light and shade of the forest at the edge of the *maidan*. Then another. There was a crackling of fallen branches, two tigers roared, repeatedly.

Slowly, regally, the two tigers crossed the road, moved into the tall, plumed grass. And vanished.

Back in the Lodge, over lunch, we were told the story about a tigress which had been hit by a jeep. Enraged, she had leapt into it. The driver had thrown himself out and grabbed it by the tail, trying to prevent it from attacking his wife. The tigress had turned on him, snarling. He had prayed to the tiger deity and let go of the tiger's tail. The animal had bounded into the jungle and vanished.

"Is there a shrine to tigers?" we asked.

"Yes, it's there near the road. People believe that tigers protect the forest. In the old days the forest gave them fodder for their animals, wood, fruit, thatch. It was a major resource for them. And now that it brings in tourists, it still is."

Lord Vishnu near his spring.

An idol of a tiger.

The shrine was a plank painted with a primitive effigy of a tiger and mounted on a platform at the side of the road. It was wreathed in a garland of flowers. A herd of cattle clomped slowly past followed by a herdsman. He had a thatch of white hair and a deeply lined face.

"Is this a very old idol?" we asked the herdsman.

He nodded and said, "From my grandfather's grandfather's day. Much more. It was installed here by the sadhus who then lived in the forest before the government took it over."

In the afternoon round we visited the caves in which sadhus had once lived. A jackal slinked past. A mongoose shimmered up and began to dine on the carcass of a langur. We drove up into a wooded hillock. There, a long boulder had been superbly sculpted into Vishnu lying on the coils of sheshnag. A spring of clear water flowed over the Preserver, fell into a masonry pool, and then poured down the hill as a stream that watered the forest. It captured an image that still glows bright and clear in our minds.

In our country, where there are still citizens who go hungry every night, we have been able to set aside many thousands of square kilometres to protect our forests, our future and our wildlife: including the endangered tiger. These become centres of environmental renewal, spreading their seeds and their benign influence to the areas around them. In marked contrast, in many of the nations of the self-styled developed world, they keep felling their forests and polluting the atmosphere. They have butchered most of their wildlife and refer to the rest as 'game' fit only to be hunted and slaughtered for sport.

We, happily, still have the perennially recharging sanity of our forests.

Before the Monks

AJANTA

We looked beyond the paintings.

We know that the caves are famed for their Buddhist murals and sculptures and they draw visitors in their thousands from all over the world. The UNESCO has listed them as part of the heritage of the world. They have been filmed, photographed, written about and discussed in learned seminars by artists, archaeologists, sculptors and historians. Nevertheless we believe that, in spite of all this exposure for more than two centuries, a few essential, unanswered questions remain.

We went looking for some of these answers on a pleasant spring day in Maharashtra.

The caves have been cut in a horseshoe shaped cliff in the valley of the Waghora River. We drove up to the view point at the

The span of the sculpted cliff of Ajanta.

Graffiti scratched in a cave— 'John Smith, 28 April 1819, Cavalry'.

edge of the escarpment from where cavalry officer John Smith, out hunting wild boar with his friends, had glimpsed a superbly carved entrance in the face of the cliff below. That was on the 29th of April, 1819 and when he and his hunting party rode down to the river, and scrambled up to the cave, they found, to their amazement, that there were many caves excavated into the volcanic rock. Pushing aside the bushes and creepers that had covered the mouths of the caves, treading carefully for fear of snakes, and dodging the flocks of bats that their hastily lit Lucifer matches had disturbed, they were astounded to see that the walls of the caves were covered in paintings as bright as if they had been done yesterday. Edward Balfour, Officer in Charge of the Government Central Museums in 1851, wrote in his definitive *Encyclopaedia Asiatica*:

> AJUNTA. The natives call the caves Yerrula, the same with those which Europeans call Ellora. They call them also Lena, and both terms mean drawings or paintings. They furnish a continuous narrative of Buddhist Art for 800 years, from about BC 200 to AD 500.

The dates have been revised by modern research but the art in the caves continues to enthral everyone who visits Ajanta: as it did us.

We left our car at the parking lot. Private vehicles are not permitted to drive beyond this point and so we boarded a shuttle bus. From the base of the cliff, a flight of steps rose to the level of the road serving the caves. Most visitors trudged up. A photographer, waving his official permit to use his cameras, hired a porter to carry his equipment. *Palki* bearers looked expectantly at the tourists pouring out of the shuttle buses. Their *palki*s are sedan chairs carried by four bearers and they ferry their passengers for the entire 550 metre length of the 29 caves, and back. Very few visitors step into all the caves: not all are worth seeing. We chose the most interesting caves relying on our guide and the excellent booklet produced by the Archaeological Survey of India.

The booklet, couched in delightfully Victorian language influenced by the writings of the old British archaeologists, said:

> It is not known under whose initiative or patronage the nucleus of these monastic aeries sprouted, but behind the selection of the spot was at work an artistic mind, keenly appreciative of the beauties of nature.

This is odd, because Cave No. 10, the very first cave to be excavated, has an inscription which says that the façade was donated by Vasisthiputra Katahadi. Two other donors have had their names written inside the cave. Judging from the script used, the cave had been dug out in the beginning of the second century BC. It's a fairly large cave with a horse-shoe shaped *chaitya* window, because it was a shrine rather than a *vihara*-residence, and it held the largest stupa in Ajanta.

A chaitya *prayer hall in Ajanta dominated by a stupa.*

A dream of the Buddha's mother painted in Ajanta.

Interestingly, the older paintings in this cave are the world's first Buddhist paintings.

Sadly, these are not in a very good state because they had been scratched by graffiti-scribbling visitors over the decades. One of them was:

John Smith
25th April 1819
Cavalry

The discoverer of the caves had left his mark!

We used our small LED torch and peered at an old painting. It depicted a king and his entourage visiting the Bodhi tree and a stupa. In those early years of the religion, Buddha was never shown in human form because he was against being deified. The Bodhi tree was one of his symbols, the stupa was another. At that time, Buddhism was a very austere, philosophical, faith which did not offer the warmth and variety that Brahmanism did. It was called Hinayana: the Little Vehicle.

To widen its reach, Buddhism became more liberal, accepting beliefs and practices that had a greater emotional appeal than a strictly intellectual one. This gave rise to Mahayana and the rich lore of the Jataka Tales said to be stories about the earlier, and also the next, incarnations of the Buddha. With such a wide canvas to draw upon, the folklorists had a field day. They created fables like the ones about the time that the Buddha had been born as Sama, the sole supporter of his blind parents. Or the other that tells of the Buddha being incarnated as a six-tusked royal elephant named Chhaddanta. Both the Sama Jataka and the Chhaddanta Jataka have been illustrated in this, the very first of the Ajanta caves, and they belong to the fourth century AD and were painted over the older ones.

In fact most of the magnificent paintings in Ajanta seem to have some reference to a Jataka tale though this often calls for a great stretch of the imagination.

Depictions of loving couples, below a row of religious figures.

For instance, the uppermost panel in the doorway of Cave 17, made a century later, shows seven Buddhas and Maitreya, the Future Buddha, sitting under their Bodhi trees. Below them, however, are eight loving couples: a rather strange mural in a monastery for celibates who have renounced the world.

This cave has so many paintings inside that the ASI booklet devotes more than 14 pages to them. One of the paintings illustrates the conquest of Sri Lanka by an Indian prince. As often happened in the past, the original inhabitants are painted as monsters and the figures of the Bodhisattvas, the humans destined to become Buddhas, are full of grace. In this shrine, the Bodhisattvas Padmapani and Vajrapani are shown as attendants to the Buddha. There are also paintings of many beautiful women, some with turbans and jewellery, another gazing at herself in a mirror and attended by two maids and a child. In a panel called a 'palace scene' a dark complexioned man holds a fair woman on his lap, in a bedroom, while three other women look on expectantly. At this time the Vataka dynasty from Andhra ruled Ajanta.

We found an inexplicable dichotomy in the art of Ajanta. On the one hand was the teeming, often overtly sensuous, depictions of the Jataka tales. On the other was the powerful serenity and detachment radiated both by the idols of the Buddha and the high ceilings, towering pillars and massive stupas of

the *chaityas*. They belonged to two different worlds. But if their creators intended to convey the message that people needed to shed the allure of everyday life and raise themselves to a Buddha-like detachment, the transition from one lifestyle to the other was not shown. Gautama Buddha shunned all extremes and preached the virtue of the Middle Way. There was no via media here.

We started looking at Ajanta from another angle.

Before the British had discovered the caves and the ASI had taken them in hand, each cave had its own access to the river, not to the other caves. Moreover, the floors of the caves are at different levels. If the caves had been created to house an order of Buddhist monks and their shrines, they would have been linked to each other. Had the caves, then, been excavated by individuals for some other purpose? But if that was the case, then their excavators would have had to spend a great deal of time and effort to chisel into the hard, volcanic, rock of the black cliff which would have not been worthwhile unless such excavations yielded a high return.

The rock gave us a clue.

According to the ASI, 'the caves are cut out of the amygdaloidal trap rock': congealed lava with hollow chambers lined with crystals which could be agate and amethyst. We recalled that the parking lot was near the MTDC Shopping Plaza where we had visited the shops of Ajanta Agate Traders. They had a huge display of these

Above: An un-monastic carving.
Left: Semi-precious stones in volcanic bubbles.

Left: Richly painted ceilings.
Below: The so-called 'Black Princess' on a monastery's wall.

volcanic 'bubbles' glittering with crystals including the attractive moss agate. According to the owner, S.H. Razique, they still find such crystals in the cliffs of Ajanta. We now asked his son, Syed Abraar Husain, who had been our guide, if he had seen such crystals in the caves. Yes, he had: at the entrance of the locked Cave 8 and on the ceilings of Caves 12 and 6. He also told us that, according to a local belief, the Buddhist monks had originally lived in a place called Lenapur. They had been persuaded to shift from there to the caves after the rulers of this area had transformed these former gem mines into *vihara*s and *chaitya*s for the monks.

Since neither the Satavahanas nor their successors the Vatakas were Buddhists, they must have had some other strong reason to spend so much time and effort on the caves.

The famous stone carved door of Ajanta.

Ajanta was near a popular trade route between the Arabian Sea and China. The continued prosperity of the kingdom depended on the popularity of this caravan route. That required the creation of transit facilities, particularly accommodation and first aid for the traveller. Monasteries, all over the world, have been associated with caring for wayfarers.

We believe that the rulers and rich merchants of Ajanta invested time and money in the caves to induce the monks to occupy them so that they, in turn, could minister to the caravanners. At that time, according to contemporary Chinese travellers, Buddhism was on the decline. There could not have been many monks is Lenapur. There was, however, a great deal of accommodation in the lavishly decorated *vihara*s because they also catered to rich and weary visiting merchants in need of physical and mental refreshment. Then, 'detoxified and de-stressed', they felt fit to enter the trading pit again. Ajanta served the same purpose that unwinding getaways do today. It was a good investment.

Or, as an inscription in Cave 26 expressed it:

> Why should not a monument be raised by those possessing wealth, desirous of mundane happiness and also of liberation?

Stellar Voyager

LONAR

A star landed here.

It was a small star: just 60 m wide, weighing about a million tonnes, but it landed with a 6 megaton bang which left an enormous hole in the ground. We stood on the rim of its crater and looked down. Water had collected in the crater, a lake had formed. It looked like a huge blue-green eye, sometimes emerald, sometimes amethyst, sometimes glazed as clouds filmed the sky. It was magnetic and had drawn us back for the third time.

We were in Maharashtra's Lonar trying to reconstruct in our minds, once again, the cataclysmic events that had rocked this place 50,000 years ago.

Behind us a board that had been erected by the Geological Survey of India proclaimed:

> LONAR CRATER
> The only hyper-velocity natural impact crater in basaltic rock in the world.

The 'green eye' of the Lonar Crater.

Above: The revered Gomukh tank.
Below: The Gomukh Temple on the rim of the crater.

It had all started in the cold darkness of outer space. "In the vast spaces between the planets," wrote astronomer Carl Sagan in *Cosmos*, "there are many objects, some rocky, some metallic, some icy, some composed partly of organic materials. They range from grains of dust to irregular blocks the size of Nicaragua or Bhutan. And sometimes, by accident, there is a planet in the way."

Within the crater a stream greens the lower slopes.

Our planet was in the way that fateful day. The rocky meteor was snared by the gravity of the earth, flamed like a rocket with the friction of our atmosphere, and hurtled down heading for the spot where we were standing now. There were forests and grasslands, here, with scattered groups of hunter-gatherers living in rock-shelters and animal-hide tents. They must have cringed and gibbered in fear as a ball of incandescence appeared in the sky and grew and grew. Animals fled, white-eyed and foam-speckled. Great trees toppled in showers of earth and crackling branches as a searing heat hit them. There was no sound from the fearful meteorite because it was rushing in at super-sonic speed preceded by an enormous shock-wave of flaming gas. When it hit, the earth melted and vapourised. A gigantic plume of lava and rocks spouted out, then cascaded down just as a monstrous sonic boom exploded and a roaring, singeing, wind, swept in flattening and scorching everything in its path. Flocks of birds popped and exploded like firecrackers in the turbulent air. Great fissures opened in the ground swallowing everything in their paths. When it had stilled and the aftershocks no longer trembled, the acrid smell of death rose from the scorched and tortured earth. For many months after that, the sky remained covered in a dust haze till successive rains cleared them and water began to fill the deep hole where the meteorite had created its crater and plunged deep into it and a chunk of it had sheared off, flipped out, landed beyond the rim and thrown up its own little crater.

The terrifying events of that day had been branded indelibly into the racial memories of our distant ancestors. It would be passed down from generation to generation around their campfires and hearths till the tale became a legend, a myth, an awesome religious experience, an apocryphal part of a folkloric record that would be repeated and treasured and embroidered in every telling but seldom understood till, in our day, scientists began to work in this star-wounded place.

Around the lake a forest of trees cools the banks.

We put our imaginations on hold, brought our minds back to the present, and picked our way, very gingerly, down a coiling, winding, rocky road into the depths of the Lonar Crater. The narrow path had changed since we had first clambered down. It had become more difficult over the years, but the lure of Lonar was so great that we had to attempt this hazardous descent once again.

The crater is shaped like a balloon with its nozzle on the north-eastern end along the entry track of the blazing meteor. The rushing star, speeding at 20 km a second, gouged out the earth below, left a ravine leading into the crater. The body of this ballooning crater is 1,830 m in circumference, and about 140 m from the rim to the water level. It slopes down steeply at first, then eases off. Close to the rim, the vegetation covering its inner surface is coarse grass and scrub. But this gradually gives way to trees and bushes, getting thicker and thicker as the bowl of the crater curves inwards.

Reassuringly, the trail now began to coil and wind like a leisurely serpent. We paused to catch our breaths and get a bird's eye view of the first temple in the crater: a star-shaped one. We scrambled down further, loose stones and gravel falling from under our feet. We were now at the edge of the heavy undergrowth. And trees began to rise just beyond. Another temple, a hidden and ruined one, emerged. This was a Shiva shrine with many of the stones of its old walls lying in tumbled scree.

We left these temples behind us and went further down. Suddenly, the terrain changed dramatically. We were in the cool shadow area of the rim. The soil was soft and loamy underfoot. We stood in a forest of tall trees: teaks, *gulmohur*, rain trees, plenty of neem, eucalyptus, silk cotton, clumps of bamboo, masses of lantana and custard apple. Rills ran chortling through it and women sat near the little, sparkling streams, washing clothes. Some of the water cascaded into a pond at the side of which there was an electric pump beating like a racing heart. A man gazed at it apprehensively as if he expected it to go into cardiac arrest at any moment. He informed us, rather distractedly, that the pump supplied water to a school at the rim of the crater.

We looked around. There was a field ahead, with cattle plodding phlegmatically. A path, with the faint aroma of mushrooms and damp earth, emerged at the edge of the lake. We had read about this lake. Water fed into it, brought down by the rills, but there was no exit except by evaporation and so, over the centuries, it had become saline. Geologists also believed that there were subterranean thermal springs, pumping more salts and minerals into the water. A man carrying an axe walked towards us and nodded politely.

"Are there any fish in this lake?" we asked.

He shook his head. "No fish, some small worms and snails and creatures like that in the shallows. That's what the birds eat. And some grass and green things. Near the shore the water is fresher. In the middle it is too brackish."

"Has it ever dried?"

"We have never seen it. But some of the old people say that once it dried and they saw strange things at the bottom."

The shallow fringes of the lake clearly hold food for foraging birds.

One of the crater's living temples.

"What strange things?"

"Like very tiny bits of broken glass and some self-formed Shivlings sticking up. They said that if the birds ever leave then that is a sign that the lake will dry and we should leave too. But that won't happen soon because, every year the level of the water rises. You will see that some trees at the edge are dying because the water has covered their roots. Also there is a temple ahead where a puja is going on. Only one of these temples still has puja." He nodded and walked on.

He had said a lot of very interesting things. So many that we felt that he might have picked up some information from the teams of geologists that had visited Lonar on their field trips. The heat and impact of meteorites hitting the ground often fuse sand into tiny bits of glass called tektites. The 'Shivlings' could have been cone formations which, from what we've read, are also found on the floors of meteoric craters.

The Crater Lake stretched before us. Greensward spread around its shores, a lone thorn tree stood in the water. The air was full of twittering whistles as water-birds dived and paddled, skimmed in spraying chevrons over the water and soared above in wheeling, circling, squadrons. If there are no fish in this lake then the shallows must be rich in other aquatic life to attract the birds. The fact that they feel secure in this protected environment would not be enough to keep them here.

Around a curve rose the Devi Temple: a fairly tall structure on a high stone plinth. On our first visit to Lonar we had met the priestess: Sunita Ramdass Dutone. She had a reputation as a seer and had been advising one of her

The legends surrounding this goddess could reflect the ancient impact.

clients in a high, chanting, monotone. When the séance was over we had spoken to her. She had said, "The devi, Kamalja, killed a ferocious demon, Lonasur, here and that's how this lake came to be." This time, however, the pujari was Chandrakala, a distant relative of Sunita who had died in the intervening years. He had a different legend to account for Lonar. According to him, the vicious Lonasur had lived in the crater and had harassed the sages who had their hermitages in the forests around. They appealed to the gods who responded by thrusting him into this depression. Before he was incarcerated, however, he made two requests: he wanted to drink water and he wanted to have his name remembered. The gods brought a stream of the Ganga here to quench Lonasur's thirst, and they named the crater Lonar.

Over the years the details of the Lonasur legend had changed but one essential fact had remained. At the bottom of this crater was buried a terrifying monster. Folk memory had retained the essential truth.

We strode around much of the 3.5 km shores of the lake, passed other ruined temples and climbed back to the rim, roughly following the ravine that the falling star had cauterised on its searing plunge into the crater.

We had been down in the crater for four hours and when we sat in the observation room of the Tourist Bungalow the crater lake stretched below us, touched by the low evening sun. We skimmed through an interesting booklet written by Sudhakar T. Bugdane. It was full of excerpts from professional papers and other information about Lonar. According to the author, though the lake is too saline for fish to survive, a few biologists have made some interesting discoveries in that mineral-rich water. Prof. Mahesh Chavdar of Yashwantrao Chavan College, Karad has, reportedly, discovered bacteria with micro-magnetic granules enabling them to float in a magnetic field. Then the 'National Cell Institute' has found an 'anti-radiation bacteria in the salt water of Lonar Lake'. Bugdane adds, 'Similarly, Dr. Yogesh Shaoche and Dr. Colin Marel of Warwick University, Britain, have discovered "Methane eating bacteria" in their research'.

We recalled the words of Dr. Carl Sagan that some meteorites are composed partly of organic materials. Did those organic materials also carry alien life-forms when Lonasur came blazing in 50,000 years ago?

When we looked up from Bugdane's booklet, the sun set, and the crater was plunged into darkness. But the cyclopean eye of the lake glistened eerily, gazing into the star-spangled womb of space.

The Fusion Seer

SHIRDI

He was a bridge.

We discovered this when we stood in a queue with hundreds of his devotees. He had renounced everything: his family, his past, his worldly possessions. And yet, all around us was the great complex that his mystique had created. Slowly the winding queue entered the place where his grave had become a shrine-mausoleum. At the far end, framed in a golden arch was the sanctum. We inched forward, came closer and closer, and then we were at the railed platform built around his grave. Rising behind and above the grave was his statue seated on a gold throne. It depicted a frail man with a clipped and grizzled beard draped in the robes of a mendicant. Its head was covered in a tightly bound piece of red cloth concealing the hair. We have referred to it as a statue in accordance with the beliefs of Islam. Here, however, it was being worshipped as an idol. Four priests in red robes sat on the platform, ministering to the devotees as they brought their offerings up to the sanctum and the image of the person they venerated.

The person had been a Muslim. The priests, the rituals, and the majority of his devotees were Hindus. This was the continuing enigma of Shirdi.

When we emerged from the shrine, we spoke to many of the pilgrims in the open

A golden tower rises above the sanctum of the Sai Baba Temple.

The sanctum of Shirdi with Sai Baba's grave in the foreground.

court in front of the temple and then to the amiable Dr. Yashwantrao Mane, Deputy Executive Officer of the Shri Sai Baba Sansthan Trust (Shirdi). We also bought a well-researched book, *Unveiling the Enigma* by Dr. Marianne Warren. But the more we probed the more we were mystified by the identity of the saint of Shirdi.

No one was sure when or where he had been born, the identity of his parents, what his parents' religion had been, where he had lived till the age of 16, or even what his name was. In spite of this, from the time the people of Shirdi village discovered him, sitting in a ruined mosque, dressed like a fakir, they were captivated by his serene, magnetic, presence. They brought him food, as they would to any ascetic, and returned home strangely at peace with themselves and their world. So, because they had to give him a name, they used a term drawn from the Persian word for a wandering religious mendicant, *sa'ih*, shortened to *Sai*, and added the honorific for a revered person, baba.

In the years that followed, the growing aura of Sai Baba completely transformed Shirdi.

Years ago, it had been a village drawing a few hundred devotees. Now, as more and more people sought relief from their cares in an increasingly troubled world, Shirdi has grown into a bustling pilgrim town with luxury hotels, restaurants and thriving shops. We recognised the dress and accents of people from all over India. The restaurants catered to their varied tastes: robust nans from the north, idli-dosa from the south; *pao-bhaji* from the west and *luchis* from the east. At an eclectic breakfast of corn flakes and the spiced puffed rice *poha* from Maharashtra, we gazed through the glass walls of our restaurant and saw a herd of cattle plodding down the main street of the town while a BMW, two luxury coaches, and a motley group of pilgrims waited patiently for the cows and black buffaloes to cross. The village still exists amid all the hurrying emblems of modernity. But everywhere, even in the taxis, buses and autorickshaws, there are images of that slim, lightly-bearded man, wearing a scarf on his head, a kurta over his lungi, his right leg resting on his left knee, gazing directly into the camera with a serene, slightly quizzical, look on his face.

Above: Visitors in the shopping arcade of Shirdi.
Below: Modern hotels rise on Shirdi's main road.

Left: Venerating Sai Baba's portrait. Below: The fire started by Sai Baba and kept burning ever since.

This is how he was sitting as a teen-aged boy and how he was seen as a young man, after disappearing mysteriously for some years and then, as mysteriously, reappearing in the ruined mosque. Some say he had sought solitude in the forests, preparing himself for his ministry. Jesus had done that, before he had become the Christ; so had Prince Gautama before he had become the Buddha so, too, had many other spiritual leaders. It seems to be an essential step in the development of a Great Soul, a Maha-*Atma*. After that step comes the Miracle Stage. Sai Baba is said to have admitted that miracles are necessary to attract people to his message.

The miracles continue to this day, according to the growing numbers of his devotees. The greatest miracle of Shirdi, however, is the intangible one: the continuing reconciliation of seeming contradictions. There is absolutely no doubt that Sai Baba was a Muslim mystic of one of the Sufi schools. His original appearance, lifestyle, and habits indicate this very clearly. The mosque in which he had first appeared has been carefully restored and is

Right: A statue of the Baba cooking.
Below: The dining hall at Shirdi.

still called a masjid, a mosque. And yet, as we saw, he is worshipped by Hindu priests in Hindu rituals: the traditions of two faiths co-existing in unquestioned harmony.

We joined a group of his devotees and waited for a priest to pull aside a grill behind which the fire, that Sai Baba had lit, still flamed, tended with great devotion by his followers. The ash from this fire is honoured as consecrated *bhasma* in the Hindu tradition, held to be very efficacious in warding off impending evil. Once again we were reminded of our own tradition of having penitential ash put on our foreheads at the start of our season of mourning, Lent. In fact, that day is called Ash Wednesday.

In an anteroom to the place where the fire is kept burning were the utensils and a symbolic sack of grain reminding visitors that the saint had used the fire to cook, on special occasions, huge quantities of the Sufi banquet called a *bhandara* made of mutton, rice and dal, which he would then distribute to his devotees. This practice has inspired the creation of the Sai Prasadalaya: the enormous refectory building of the Trust. Everyone who enters this charitable facility is reminded of its origins. There is a large statue of Sai Baba stirring a huge cauldron dominating the gardens of the Prasadalaya.

Now, however, in deference to the traditions of the majority of his followers, the food served in the refectory is strictly vegetarian. Traditions, however, do not govern the methods of cooking. Enormous solar collectors rise on the roof of the building like giant dish antennae and feed heat to the world's largest solar powered kitchen. It is immaculately clean, humming, bubbling, hissing and winking with its computerised panels. Its stainless steel vats, boilers and automated puri cutting, frying and chapatti baking machines, make it look like the galley of some futuristic Star Ship Bharat on an interstellar voyage.

We spoke to senior cook Kardele Prahlad. On an average day they cook 2,500 kgs of rice, 600 quintals of *toor dal* and enormous quantities of seasonal vegetables. When we marvelled at his 21st century facilities he said, "It is all due to the grace of Baba."

That was a reply that we would get repeatedly in Shirdi from the employees of the Trust, the traders, coach drivers, restaurateurs, and certainly every pilgrim we spoke to. To them Sai Baba is still alive though his mortal remains may lie in his shrine.

In the offices of the great dining building, officials kept a careful watch over the streams of pilgrims buying the ten rupee coupons for a meal in the huge refectory. This is communicated electronically to the kitchen so that fresh food is always ready when the next batch of 2,000 diners sit down at the tables and armies of servers fill their stainless-steel platters. When one batch of diners rises the clearance is swift, floors are washed down, mechanised cleaning machines, like the ones used in airports, swab and dry them, another array of gleaming platters are laid on the tables, and the next batch is admitted. Of the 50,000 pilgrims who visit the religious complex every day, 30,000 sit down to dine in successive batches. And there is a separate section for those who cannot afford to pay even the very nominal ten rupees.

Clearly, the Trust receives a great deal of money. Equally obviously, this is used to improve facilities for all who visit Shirdi. The Sansthan has built, and manages, hostels to suit most pockets. Judging by the experience of our family, they are run with as much attention to the passengers' needs as upscale hotels are.

A beautifully designed guest house managed by the Sai Baba Trust.

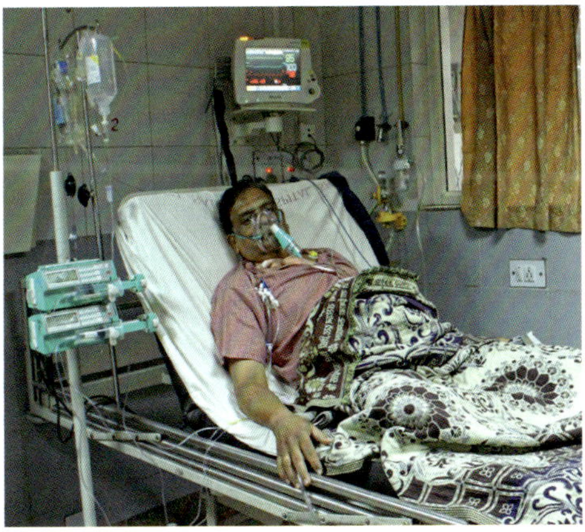

Then there is the Trust's Multi-Speciality Hospital. In the hospital's atrium, some of the families of the patients stood in a circle singing bhajans. When they had finished, a delicate-featured woman with pepper-and-salt hair and wearing her sari tied in the Maharashtrian way, spoke to us. She said her son-in-law had had open-heart surgery yesterday and now he is well on the way to complete recovery. Then she added a phrase that had become very familiar to us. "It's all due to the grace of Baba." We heard that phrase again from Cardiac Surgeon Vidyut Kumar Sinha. When he had joined in 2006, they had done three surgeries a month, now the five cardiac surgeons do fifty to sixty operations every month. They have done surgery on the youngest open-heart patient in the world: a fourteen-year-old boy and their recovery rate is 98%. We learnt, later, that the world recovery rate on such operations is 95%.

Wearing sterile gowns and masks we entered the Intensive Care Unit and met Jowar Srirang Nandlal twenty four hours after he had had open-heart surgery. He nodded to us cheerfully, allowing us to take his photograph. His nurse said, "He's recovering well: it's all due to the power of Baba!" Jowar nodded emphatically again.

We returned to the shrine complex, visited the very simple rooms where the Baba had slept and the neem tree which, according to the security guard, the Baba had regarded as his guru. This, however, is probably where Sai Baba had buried his mentor as, apparently, is the custom among Sufi seers.

All this, however, left us with a major unanswered question. Sai Baba had not amassed any personal wealth, he did not have any political ambitions, he had not even left any documents specifying his philosophy. In fact this

Above: A patient recovering from open-heart surgery in Shirdi's hospital.
Right: Pilgrims near the temple.

A monument to the Baba's guru under a spreading neem tree.

huge, efficient organisation had been created by his devotees many years after his death. But how has the charisma of this unassuming Sufi seer, who has not left behind any specific teachings or anointed successors, continued to exercise such a hold on an increasing number of devotees so many decades after his death? The only explanation for this burgeoning phenomenon came from Dr. Marianne Warren's book. According to her, Sufi mystics believe that there has always been a structured hierarchy of enlightened humans who oversee the affairs of the universe, protecting it from harm. They have existed in every age and, as one gives up his life, his successor takes over. The head of this organisation of mystic guardians, imbued with enormous authority, is called the *qutb-e-irshad*.

Sai Baba, she contends, was the *qutb* of his age.

For those who believe that, we would like to correct the first sentence of this chapter. We had started by saying 'He was a bridge'. We should have put that in the present tense.

For his estimated million devotees, living in a world riven by sectarianism, terrorism as well as divisive bigotry, Sai Baba is a faith-spanning bridge to sanity.

The Saga of the Tiffin Carriers

THE DABBAWALAS

They are unique to Mumbai.

No other city in the world has them because no other city has the special characteristics of this booming, bustling, Big Apple of India. For one thing Mumbai, aka Bombay, stretches along a narrow neck of land thrusting out from the mainland into the Arabian Sea. As it grew from a low-lying,

A dabbawala *jogs with his laden tray.*

Lunch packets in a variety of marked dabbas.

mangrove-girt, trading colony to the industrial and financial hub of modern India, land prices skyrocketed and still continue to soar. This makes it virtually impossible for the average employee to live near his place of work in the high-rises and glittering towers of south Mumbai. Moreover, Mumbai is a great magnet. It draws people from all over India, and from all our myriad castes, creeds and communities. Each one of them has its own dietary foibles and taboos. Besides, as the cost of living in Mumbai soared, it became increasingly difficult to get one's meals from downtown eateries every working day. And since we Indians have not, as yet, taken to sandwiches, salads and cold-cuts or even cold food in general, the great army of Mumbai's workers were left with just two options.

Starve all through the working day, or dream of having someone deliver your hot, home-cooked, meal at your office. An impossible dream? But then, Mumbai is a city where many impossible dreams have become reality. As this one did.

Enter the *dabbawala*s.

As former Mumbaikars, we had seen these food couriers hustle on board our commuter trains, rush off at terminuses and trot through crowded roads carrying coffin-sized crates laden with lunches. They were as much a part of the Mumbai scene as the yellow cabs with black tops. Mumbaikars are street-smart, slick and always alert for the main chance. They have been that way from 1890 at least. It was in that year that an old Parsi lady in the suburb of Dadar spoke to Mahadu Iwhaji Bacha. She wanted him to help her to get a tiffin carrier across to her husband who worked in the commercial heart of Bombay, as it was called then.

For those who were not familiar with the term tiffin carrier, Nigel B. Hankin's excellent Hanklyn-Janklin *defines it as:*

> *A nest of several circular containers in which the courses of a meal can be carried on a journey or to the office.*

That was the start of the *dabbawala*s. From those humble beginnings this self-made Indian organisation has grown into a huge network whose incredible efficiency has won the admiration of international business schools and even of Prince Charles of England.

On a humid day in March, to the crash of the carrier-laden crates, called 'trays', being deposited on the pavement, the clang of tiffin carriers being sorted out office-wise, and the announcements of arriving and departing trains echoing out of the station, we spoke to the stocky President of the Mumbai Tiffin Box Suppliers Association, Sopan Laxman Mare, the tall and articulate Kiran Govind Gavande, a member of the Association, and other members who chimed in, occasionally, with their remarks like the one about Elvis Presley.

"How many *dabbawala*s are there today?"

"3,500 plying the Western Railway; 1,500 on the Central Railway. This station, Churchgate, is on the Western Railway. We have two lakh customers, and they're growing."

"Really? In spite of fast food eateries?"

"Chhah! You can't live on fast foods. See what happened to that singer Pressy...that Elbis Pressy!"

"What time do you pick up the food?"

"The earliest is at 8:00 in the morning. If it is not ready we leave but we give that lady one more chance. The next time it is delayed we remove her from our list. We deliver to the office by 1:00 pm sharp, or earlier. We collect

Dabbas *in a tray as they arrive at Churchgate Station.*

by 2:00 pm. If late we leave. Again only one more chance. We deliver empty tiffin boxes to housewives by 5:30 in the evening latest. We charge about 500 rupees a month per customer."

Added Baburam, "I collect tiffin carriers from 20 flats in Andheri: that's far away!"

"How many fit into a tray?"

"Forty to forty-five. A laden tray weighs 85 to 100 kilos. And there are five changing points where we offload the trays from the train, change them into other trays, and then change them again. It has all to be done very fast, very accurately."

"How do you know which tiffin carrier goes into which tray?"

"We have alpha-numerical markings on every tiffin carrier indicating the location of the flat, the changing points, the delivery points, the *dabbawala*s involved."

"Who worked out this system for you?"

"We did. Can your MBAs do it? Never! In fact they have often asked us to explain it to them. Even Prince Charles did. We sent him a present for his wedding and we have a letter from him to prove it. Our system is flawless."

Above: Every dabba *has an identifying code. Below:* Dabbas *transported in hand-carts.*

"How old is the oldest *dabbawala*?"

"That's Bikaji. He's 74 years old and he's been working for 50 years. The youngest is 21."

We watched fascinated as the trays arrived and were sorted out into hand-drawn carts, cycles, and even festooned like multiple garlands around the necks and shoulders of delivery *dabbawala*s. We learnt that all *dabbawala*s are put through a rigorous training because they have to deal courteously with housewives and so they cannot be uncouth or drunk. Moreover if they forget to wear their distinguishing white caps, they are initially fined for the first offence and then removed from the Association if it should happen again.

They run a very tightly controlled, disciplined, organisation.

We left the *dabbawala*s to get on with their delivery schedules and walked across to the Tea Centre for our own lunch. In the lobby, next to the lift, we noticed a *dabba* under a trestle table. The guard told us that

Above: Members of the Dabbawalas' *Committee. Right:* Dabbawalas' *also use cycles*

Dabbawalas *distributing food containers among delivery men.*

it belonged to someone in the Synthetic & Rayon Textiles Export Promotion Council on an upper floor. We went up and met E.L. Paulo, Director and Secretary of SRTEPC.

He lived in the suburbs, on Mira Road, and he had been dealing with the *dabbawalas* for ten years. He told us that they pick up his tiffin carrier at 8:00 every morning.

"In all these ten years," he said, "they have never missed. It's a wonderful service. Very reliable."

That coming from a senior executive of an export promotion council, who deals with international standards as a matter of course, is a great endorsement. This is particularly commendable when it has been applied to a network as wide-ranging and as entirely grass-roots generated as Mumbai's unique *dabbawala*s.

And if you want another endorsement, ask Prince Charles.

Retro Station

MATHERAN

Here, there are no cars.

It's the expressed will of this small town's people, reaffirmed generation after generation without compromise. This greenest hill-station in our land is a beloved old friend: we laid the foundations of our team in Matheran, another incarnation ago. It is still extraordinarily well wooded. On this, our fifth visit, we hoped to find out what makes the people of Matheran keep their little town so unspoilt when the other hill-stations of India were being blighted by, so-called, developers.

An old mansion, now 'The Verandah in the Forest' of the Neemrana Group.

A rickshaw in a green tunnel in Matheran.

We parked our car at Dasturi Naka then made a dash in the rain up a red and unpaved road into the warmth of our room in an old Raj-era bungalow. If we closed our eyes, we could almost see men with mutton-chop whiskers and stern expressions, and women with cinched waists and skirts with floor-sweeping trains. In that serene, old world, atmosphere we slept like logs.

Birdsong woke us. That, and the sun bounding onto our windowsill like a fluffy, ginger kitten, purring in this 803 m high place in the Western Ghats. We have, in the past, walked around the town and also explored it on horseback. This morning, we decided to sit in hand-pulled rickshaws and do a nostalgic tour of "The Wood"...*Mathe*..."At the Top"...*Ran*. Our rickshaws creaked through tunnels of green enriched with the aroma of damp earth and growing things. Such jungle journeys are a wonderful part of the Matheran experience. This little town sits on a densely wooded plateau and its main attractions are a number of 'points' at the edge of the escarpment giving horizon-stretching views over the plains. Back in 1850, when it was discovered by Hugh Mallet, the Collector of Thane, an English official had noted:

> The best views are from Garbut Point in the morning, and from Panorama Point in the evening, from the latter looking down in Bombay with the broken coast and harbour, on Malabar Hill, by Mazagon and Mahim, a sight rarely equalled.

Clearly, these Britons had set the standards by which the people of Matheran still lived. Following Hugh Mallet's discovery, his colleagues had

Steep escarpments surround the plateau of the hill station.

built their cottages in Matheran to escape from the heat and humidity of the plains. They had been followed by the affluent old families of Bombay who shared their urbane tastes. They, probably, also treated it as a sanatorium for their sick and infirm. In the elegantly simple Holy Cross Catholic Church, we had seen a stone plaque saying:

Sacred to the memory of MARY
the fondly loved wife of
J.R. Denison Mackenzie Esq. FRCS
Surgeon H.M. Indian Army and Senior Surgeon
Jamsetjee Jeejeebhoy Hospital Bombay
Died in Matheran on 16th May, 1871
Aged 24 years
Requiescat in Pace

Since he was the senior surgeon in the famed JJ Hospital, he was likely to have been in his mid or late forties with a young and sick wife. He had, probably, brought her here to recoup from a serious illness or to be cured from one: malaria had been a major scourge in the low-lying soggy plains of Bombay.

Today, though Bombay-Mumbai has shed its malarial tag, it was obscured by its own industrial success: a thick, grey, haze. We were disappointed when we stood at the edge of the plateau and looked out, but when we asked honeymooners Jyoti and Rakesh if they felt let down, they smiled and Rakesh said, "We came here to get away from the noise and bustle of

Inside the peaceful Holy Cross Church.

Delhi, and this is so quiet and wooded: it's really great." Added Jyoti, "And they're such wide horizons. This is, like, too good?"

They told us that they had been to most of the 36 Points in Matheran and had been thrilled at the dizzying views of green cliffs falling away steeply and of distant blueing ranges rising beyond. We visited a few of them and managed to get three repetitive echoes for every call we bellowed from Echo Point. Charlotte Lake is always on our Point-to-Point itinerary. There were tattered scarves of mist drifting over the water and somewhere in the dense woods surrounding the lake, a Malabar Whistling Thrush streaked its silver notes. On the lake there was only the barest suggestion of ripples as if it had been covered in shimmering crepe-de-chine. No one boats or

Above: The famous Nariman Chikki shop. Below: Visitors at Echo Point.

swims here because the people of Matheran want to drink pure, unpolluted, natural water.

Which is why we wondered, this time, why there were so many vendors of mineral water in the little single-street town. Then one of them told us, "Tourists drink it because they come from places where the water is polluted. But we are old fashioned. We stick to pure Matheran water: It's best. Like our honey. And our *chikki*." *Chikki*, otherwise known as peanut brittle, is a speciality of Matheran. On an earlier visit, one of the shopkeepers had assured us that everything, including *chikki*, had been brought in from elsewhere. Now, when we visited the Nariman Chikki Mart this seemed unlikely. It's far too up-market an establishment to shy away from making something so simple as peanut brittle. We also bought *chivda* and honey from

them. Nariman is a Parsi name and Matheran seems to have always been very popular with this high-achieving community. There's an entire market constructed by a Parsi. The entrance to the market had an arch identifying it as the 'Anbai Pestonjee N. Kapadia Memorial'.

A plaque gave a more detailed explanation. It said:

This market was constructed out of funds provided by Pestonjee
Naoriji Kapadia Esq and handed to the Matheran Municipality as
a memorial to his wife Bai Ratanbai Pestonji Naoriji Kapadia
who died at Matheran on the 29th day of April 1917.
Superintendent of Matheran
Lieutenant Colonel M.P. Khereghat

Parsis are reputed philanthropists and conservationists. We had begun to see their presence behind much of the uniqueness of Matheran. The survival of the shoemakers is a case in point.

Thanks to the exclusion of cars, walking in the town and its forests is a major recreational activity and it has generated a thriving industry in hand-made footwear. These leather workers are not roadside cobblers but craftsmen marketing their products in well-established shops. Ironically, their major customers are those who would normally travel in gas-guzzling cars.

There is, however, one internal combustion engine allowed in this determinedly eco-friendly hill-station. We ambled down to the little railway terminus in the heart of the mountain town. There were long queues of

The pristine and wooded Charlotte Lake.

A traditional mochi *caters to the walkers of this hill resort.*

tourists waiting to buy tickets for the chuffing journey in the tiny train. Above the ticket counter there were portraits of two Muslim gentlemen in ceremonial attire: the late Sir Adamjee Peerbhoy who financed the railway at the staggering cost of Rs. 1,600,000 and the late Honourable Abdul Hussein Adamjee Peerbhoy who constructed the Neral-Matheran Railway between 1901 and 1907. The British had said that such a railway would not be feasible. Abdul Hussein, however, 'by his rare engineering skill', did the impossible and was thereafter known as Matheran Railwaywala.

The little locomotive which first drew this train was driven by steam. When it was retired, it was installed on its own pedestal and honoured with a plaque saying:

> Here lies the steam locomotive which moved up and down in the service of the people of Matheran for over 77 years. Manufactured in the year 1902, this has rendered service since the year 1902—the year of the opening of this section.

We boarded a compartment filled with people returning from a refreshing holiday in the little town. Exactly on time, at ten to two in the afternoon, the diesel engine howled like a lost soul, there was a jerk and then the train rolled out of Matheran, clickety-clacking on its narrow tracks. Some of our fellow travellers clapped and cheered as if they hadn't expected the locomotive to

The tough little hill train awaits passengers.

Lord Ganesh guards a difficult stretch of the track.

locomote. It was a very interesting journey. The train wound through dense woods with the trees parting occasionally to give a few, dramatic, glimpses of the plains far below. On one occasion a large image of the God of Good Beginnings, Lord Ganesh, peered down at us benignly, blessing all who passed. In his unperturbed gentleness he captured the calm pace of life in Matheran shrugging off the cares of the outside world.

We settled back in our seats contentedly and recalled some interesting facts about this railway. The total length of the line was 20.01 kms. It wound around 226 curves, crossed 122 bridges, ascended a maximum gradient of 1 in 20 and an average gradient of 1 in 25. Its maximum permissible speed was 16 kmph. Its only tunnel was known as the Kissing Tunnel because the train went through its darkness for the duration of a single kiss: more a hurriedly stolen Victorian peck than a long and lingering X-rated osculation.

Our statistical train of thought was interrupted when we stopped with a thud, groan and a jerk at a station called Aman. Then we were jolted into motion again.

We now began to chug on a dramatic thread of a line laid between a cliff and a precipice: there was a vertiginous drop below and a sheer rocky rise above. From our seats we got the impression that we were levitating down the mountain. We have travelled on the famed ratchet railways of the Alps but none of those trips have been as thrilling as this one. In those trains there was the reassuring clack! clack! of the cogged wheel in the centre of the tracks, preventing us from slipping back. Here all we had to sustain us

The Matheran train chugs down to Neral.

was faith in the engineering skill of the late Honourable Abdul Hussein Adamjee Peerbhoy.

So it was with great relief that we stopped and disembarked at Water Pipe where engines recharged their boilers in the old days of steam. A burly railway official checked everyone's tickets, herded the passengers back into the train, waved a green flag, blew a whistle, the slim, taciturn, grizzled driver got the locomotive to moan like a stricken beast before clickety-clacking his train down the track.

Mist swept in and settled cool and nostalgic around us leaving a small window of startling clarity down the track, focusing our vision. What we had been looking for began to flip through our minds, coalesced. Old tiled cottages, and the tastes of childhood: *chikki* and honey and *chivda*. Paths meandering through the moist mushroom fragrances of the forests. The silver sound of the Whistling Thrush slicing through the patter of rain on the roof. The warm texture of hand-tooled leather and the soft squelch of slush underfoot. The rocking, rolling, clickety-clacking of a toy train on a mountain track. This nostalgia is not for the BPL, or the nouveau riches, or those of the Billionaires Club. But for the stolid, solid, long-established, much maligned Middle Class such reminders of their heritage nurture the tap-roots of their stability.

Matheran, more than any other town in India, is a salute to such sterling, old, values that, clearly, have stood the test of time.

The First Line

THE SEA FORTS

They sit like ominous battleships, anchored in the bay.

But they are certainly larger than any battleship ever built, more self-reliant, can carry very much more fire-power, and they can never be sunk regardless of what their enemies do. They are fortified islands, lying offshore and controlling the seas and the shores within reach of their powerful cannon. On Maharashtra's Konkan Coast we drove to the small port of Rajpuri and visited the office of an organisation with a large name: The Janjira Paryatak Sahakari Sanstha Maryadit, which is the Rajpuri to Janjira Fort Sailing Boat Service.

The window of the office looked out across a blue bay dotted with the Service's sailing boats. Beyond them rose the dark and impressive bulk of

Boats await at the foot of the fortified island.

Festive fishing boats at a creek on the way to Janjira.

the island that had become the sea fort of Janjira. It was ringed with massive stone walls, rose to a hillock in the centre and looked as impregnable as it had proved to be. Janjira had stood as the main bastion of a sea-faring people for over 300 years.

While we waited for the officials of the Service to sell enough tickets to make the trip viable, we bought an interesting book: *History of Janjira State* by Sharad Chitnis. The author was a retired government servant, had been born in Janjira, and had access to records and other information not available to others because his family had been closely associated with the former rulers of Janjira.

These erstwhile princes, according to Chitnis, were descendants of slaves brought from Abyssinia and were known as the Siddhis. Chitnis says that most of the Siddhis:

> ...were wheat coloured with high straight noses and thin lips.

He goes on to say:

> The Abyssinian slaves were faithful, brave and energetic. They were also called *Habshi Kafirs* and often were found to be of superior quality than their masters. On the strength of their qualities and ability, they held positions of high trust.

They were also skilled seamen and so the Siddhis were appointed commanders of Janjira fort. In a short while they had used the ship building

Across a bay rises the implacable bulk of Janjira.

skills of the local community, along with the expertise of the Portuguese shipwrights of Bassein on the coast, to create a formidable fleet. In 1621, Siddhi Ambar became an independent ruler and founded the Siddhi dynasty.

At this point we closed the book, walked down to the jetty, and boarded the ferry along with a number of other visitors, and cast off. The wind hissed gently in the rigging, the sail flapped occasionally as we changed direction to avoid underwater rocks, the waves slap-slapped against the wooden hull of our boat, Janjira fort grew in our vision till its dark walls and battlements towered above us. Our ferry beached with an abrasive rasp and we quickly hopped out.

Up above, cannons thrust their snub noses through the embrasures. If we had been an attacking force we'd have been blasted out of the water soon after we cast off. And if, by some subterfuge, we had managed to reach these forbidding walls, defensive fire would have wiped us out halfway up the winding stone steps rising to the battlements. Carvings on the walls showed enormous lions decimating smaller elephants. The lion had, for many centuries, been the emblem of the Abyssinian rulers and the last king had kept lions as pets and was known as The Lion of Judah. His dynasty

Above: A cannon on the battlements. Below: Ruins of the Abyssinian Sea Fort.

Left: A significant carving on the wall of the Siddhi fort. Below: The hinterland resembles that of Goa.

claimed to be descendants of their ancestress the Queen of Sheba and the legendary King Solomon of the Jews. The elephant has always been associated with India. The message of the carvings on the walls of Janjira entrance was clear.

The Siddhi princes surrendered their domains to the Indian Union in 1948 and they seem to have abandoned Janjira. We picked our way up flights of stairs, saw huge reservoirs covered in green algae, walked under arches, past somnolent buildings decorated with intricate abstract designs carved into stone facades, disturbed cooing pigeons nesting in the eaves, bats hanging down from ancient rafters, a duck leading her ducklings into the shelter of a tree overhanging one of the ponds. On the broad battlements, rusting cannons ringed the fort in a lethal barrier.

Shivaji had attacked this fort. He had been a great military strategist and had realised that though his land-based forces could out-manoeuvre the Portuguese, Mughals and British in the coastal mountains and plains, they were no match for the naval might of the Siddhis. Unmarked headstones, in an overgrown graveyard, could have held the remains of soldiers fallen to Shivaji's attacks. But there were no signs to identify the buildings and no information boards to speak of the long history of this Indo-Abyssinian dynasty.

Above: Ferrying passengers to the mainland. Below: Shivaji's Sindhudurg Sea Fort.

A group of Class 12 students, who had sailed across in our boat, gathered around us and asked, "Is this really a very historic fort, a very important one?"

We said it was both.

"Then why has it been neglected?"

"Perhaps we have too much history," we said.

One of them smiled cynically, "Or is it because, as our Sir said, some people prefer to accept the uncertain legends of our mythical past, and conveniently forget to verify the facts of history?" His companions burst out laughing, applauding the views of an admired teacher.

The boatmen called out to us, saying that the tide was changing, so we hurried down to the landing and did not have to answer that question.

We were still thinking about it the next morning, over our typical Maharashtrian breakfast of spiced, beaten rice, called *poha*, and *udip*, a sibling of *upma*. After which we drove through a very Goan-like countryside of coconuts and cottages bright with oleander and hibiscus. We left our car in the fishing town of Malwan and walked across an aromatic beach dotted with boats. A flotilla of trawlers bobbed on the slow swell. Large outrigger boats

The little beach in the curve of the battlements, probably reserved for women.

rowed slowly across the bay. Our outrigger came alongside and we teetered across the thwarts and sat with our legs in the sloshing bilge. The outboard motor growled to life and our outrigger kept us on an even keel while sea-birds sat on sharp, spume-glistening rocks, watching our heaving progress with mild interest. The sea fort of Sindhudurg grew and the dark walls of the fort rose higher and higher out of the sea.

Then our boat snuggled its nose into the soft sand at the base of the fort's wall and we hopped ashore and trudged up the steps built into the cupping curtain wall. The fort is enormous. Our guide, Sadiq Sheikh, said that it covered 48 acres but there is not a single signboard to identify any of its historic ruins. There were, however, fields inside, and tiled cottages, owned by people who call themselves "The Servants of Shivaji."

Sadiq led us past a temple and said, "We are the descendants of the warriors and retainers of Shivaji Maharaj. My ancestors used to beat the drums warning of an attack, and also on other occasions. I still beat the ceremonial drum for the morning and evening *aarti* in the main temple and get a salary of Rs. 216 a year from the temple's annual grant of Rs. 5,000. We shall visit the temple on the way back."

We strode on, past small, tiled, cottages and fields of *bhindi* and brinjal. He pointed out the three sweet-water wells: the *doodh, dahi* and *shakar vav*s. We took his word for it that they did, indeed, taste of milk, yoghurt and sugar. He assured us that their water levels vary only very slightly year round. Then we climbed to the Jehelani Burj, the observation tower looking out over the Arabian Sea. We had a panoramic view of much of the fort with a rocky pool where women washed clothes and a small scallop of a beach accessed through a door. Here, apparently, royal ladies disported themselves under the watchful gaze of women sentries.

Clearly, Shivaji had used his military expertise to choose the location of this sea fort. Its garrison could control both the seaward and landward approaches effectively. The sentry posts on the battlements had conveniently located toilets and we also spotted what could have been guardhouses for relief sentries and stores for arms. Shivaji had, reputedly, also ensured that the foundations of the battlements were set firmly in molten lead. Like all great generals he had learnt from his military setbacks and had improved on the strategy of his enemies, the sea faring Siddhis.

Picking our way through the fields and scrub, we backtracked to the unusual Shivrajeshwar Temple. We entered through a pillared hall with the sanctum right ahead of us. On the wall to the left of us was a garlanded portrait of Shivaji. The idol in the sanctum was made of black stone and it was covered in a triangular red cloth with three lines of gold at the bottom. Devotees of Lord Shiva often identify themselves by drawing three parallel

In the temple Shivaji is worshipped as an aspect of Lord Shiva.

Above: In the Fort, a village where Shivaji's servitors settled.
Left: Shivaji's portrait in Sindhudurg.

lines on their foreheads with either sandalwood paste or sacred ash. A sword had been placed across this cloth and another sword was in a glass case at the side of the idol. We spoke to the pujari, Sriram Sakpal, and he told us that his family had been brought from Kolhapur in 1695, the year this temple had been built by Shivaji's son Raja Ram. That is also the year when the idol of Shivarajeshwar was installed by him.

The revered Shivarajeshwar is an idol of Shivaji as an aspect of Lord Shiva. It is, reputedly, the only one of its kind in the world.

Sadiq Sheikh led us back, to the main entrance of the great fort, and up a flight of stone steps to the battlements and two other, smaller, shrines. One reputedly held Shivaji's handprint; the other his footprint. While we were clambering down, Sadiq said, "Shivaji Maharaj's employees were Hindus, Christians and Muslims. In fact his first admiral was Daulat Khan." We were surprised.

We wished Sadiq Sheikh goodbye, boarded our bobbing outrigger, and pitched and rolled our way back across the bay. But now that we are writing our travel diary, something bothers us. Thanks to the salaries, decreed by Shivaji, to the Muslim and other descendants of his hand-picked retainers, the warrior-king's liberal attitude has been clearly established. That could be embarrassing to some of his self-proclaimed followers. But then, as that wise 'Sir' reportedly said, 'Some people prefer to accept the uncertain legends of our mythical past and conveniently forget to verify the facts of history.'

Clearly, in more ways than one, the Sea Forts are history.

The Festival Before the Fast

THE CARNIVAL

It's unique.

Its name explains its origin. Carnival is taken from the Latin words *carnem levare*, 'remove meat'. In those days, since meat was forbidden to Catholics during the mourning period of Lent, they would invite their friends to eat all the meat stored in their larders. These feasts grew into the Carnival.

In Asia, the traditional Carnival is celebrated in only one place: Goa.

Even here, however, it has evolved. Years ago, Goan historian Dr. Carmen Azevedo told us that the Carnival was, originally, a family festival. After the socially sanctioned raid on friends' larders and cellars, there was much singing and dancing and then the young people would throw powder on each other. That year we also spoke to Chico Fernandes, then a member of the Carnival Committee. We asked him why it had changed from a family festival to a community one. "I think I was responsible for that," Chico had admitted. As a hotelier he was looking for an acceptable activity that would bring in much needed tourist dollars. "I had some Brazilian magazines with me," Chico recalled, "and in them I saw the colour and pageantry of the Brazilian Carnivals. 'Why can't we do the same here?' I thought. And that's really how the present Carnival began."

We decided to look behind the greatest show in Goa. We drove along one of the little state's broad causeways; then turned into one of the twisting, palm-shaded, shrine-dotted roads of a typical Goan village, and stopped at a cottage workshop where one

The Goan Carnival was probably inspired by the Carnival in Brazil.

A painter busy working on a float for the Carnival.

of the Carnival's floats was being created. Such floats are an essential part of the Carnival. Whole villages, local communities and even private associations pool their resources to create the best floats. They depict current concerns often very bitingly. Corruption, political skulduggery, hypocrisy have all been targeted on Carnival floats, which is one reason why they are constructed away from prying eyes. We had to prove our bona fides as neutral observers before we were allowed to see the work in progress in that little village.

But this was no village scene. Men welded iron rods into intricate designs, frames for the giant figures which would be built on the float. Carpenters planed and sawed and hammered. Decorators cut swathes of scarlet cloth to cover the float.

Floats are generally mounted on trucks or flatbeds and often carry a live band or a hyped-up sound system playing the latest pop music. Every float is followed by its own team of intriguingly dressed mummers capturing the theme of the float, or rows of dancers moving down the street in perfect time to the music.

We left the float fabricators and headed for a graceful, old, double-storeyed, building in the capital, Panaji. It overlooked the promenade of the gently flowing Mandovi River. We had a little difficulty in making our way up the stairs to the first floor because they were crowded with young people rushing up and down and the air was full of music, conversation and laughter. In the midst of all this kaleidoscopic pandemonium, a carnival impresario sat behind a desk in a small room. He had the unflappable composure of a modern day Buddha. Behind him was a chart which listed who had to deliver what, when. The names of the dancers, descriptions of the dresses, decorations and devices were also listed. And then, in a tightly coordinated PERT diagram, they were all carefully dovetailed with each other till they came together on the morning of the great parade.

In a festive mood, Mummers liven a Carnival procession.

"All my helpers are volunteers," the impresario said. "No, we don't pay them. Excuse me...I said I wanted the dresses at four o'clock; it's now five. Yes I've sent the car for them...All these young people come here of their own accord, they work hard, and all they want is a party when the Carnival is over. Would you like to see what we're doing here?"

We walked around a warren of rooms: rooms full of masks and caps and props; rooms full of costumes; and a large hall where, to amplified music, teams of young people were dancing the way they would in the street for many kilometres, in the hot sun, during the Carnival procession.

We retreated to our hotel and met King Momo, Lord of the Carnival Revels. He is appointed every year and must be a man of impressive stature to fit into his role. He presides over the Panaji procession and as many other festivities as he can attend. During his rule, fun is the watchword.

Carnival day dawned bright and clear and the crowds began to stream in and mass on both sides of the Carnival route. The music was filling the streets when we grabbed a hurried lunch and rushed down. Both pavements on that long road were crowded and more and more spectators were jockeying for vantage points. The Governor drove up, flag flying; the honour guard snapped to attention; the Governor took the salute and sat down.

The procession began.

Even to this day it is a collage of images. Momo and his queen and courtiers and ladies-in-waiting and the guards on the royal float leading them all; a phalanx of outriders on their roaring motorcycles; music, music, music; bobbing figures, fighting figures, clowning figures; dancers, dancers, dancers, swirling, pirouetting, strutting; a Stone Age tribe attacking an enormous serpent which rolled its eyes and licked its forked tongue; a bearded mendicant with a large begging bowl and a placard around his neck asking for 'Black Money Only'; more music, music, music; fishermen

King Momo rides his chariot along with his court.

skilfully netting a giant crab which skittered all over the road; a Mexican sleeping on his back under a huge sombrero and near him a large sign saying 'Public Waste Department'; more dancers and much more music.

And so it went on and on and on for hours, winding its way down the long river promenade, around the circle, down to the great flight of steps leading to the white magnificence of Our Lady's Church. Here, in the sunset-softened evening, the Carnival procession streamed past King Momo and his court. Then, when the last of the floats and dancers and bands and mummers had gone, the crowd moved in, colourful and dense. King Momo unrolled a scroll and, with great solemnity, he read his proclamation. He ordered that there should be no sorrow or seriousness, no concern for anything but joy, festivity and happiness.

And the Goans and the Carnival visitors took his commands to heart.

From that night on, the whole of Goa went jubilant. Great balls were held, vying with each other for the best décor, the best bands, the best dancers. We danced on a beach better than a work-out; waltzed at a Fancy Dress ball yes people do know how to waltz in Goa; cavorted in a disco like sardines being shaken in a can but there we won a bottle of aromatic and powerful *Anise Liqueur*. We came home most mornings just as dawn was gilding the waters of the Mandovi.

Happily, thanks to the growing spirit of the Carnival, the old traditions are being rediscovered. One day, not too early of course, we drove off the road and attended a village fiesta. People had collected under two spreading trees leaving a clearing in the centre. On one side a band played, above them a cycle had been suspended from a branch for all to see. In the centre of the circle a local actor and his troupe were staging a satirical play. We don't understand Konkani but the crowd laughed, whistled and clapped. The band came in to underscore the most cutting parts of the dialogue, to indicate changes of scene, and between acts. The cycle was the prize for the raffle. The audience was completely spellbound by it all. "After the play," our driver said, "the boys will throw powder on the girls. The band and troupe will move on to the next village. The whole village subscribes to the show because that's part of Carnival."

We managed to rush back to our hotel just in time to change for the Red and Black Ball. This is the most famous street dance in Panaji. They cordon off the street, erect a stage for the bands on one side, canopy the street with red streamers, and insist that everyone attending wear red or black or both. Even the fancy-dress competitors must wear red and black: one creative person came as a letter box!

Dancers at the very popular Red and Black Ball.

Street dancers are an essential feature of the Carnival.

We were fairly tired by this time, but the effect of all that compulsive music, excellent Goan wines, spirited *feni*, and rich Goan fare put new life into us. Also it's quite a psychedelic experience to become part of a floor merging and shifting in a myriad patterns of black and red. After a while, reality ceased to exist and only the music and the movements were real.

But even unreality has to end. At six in the morning, the church bells pealed. People listened, looked at their watches, began to wish their friends goodbye, and started to leave. We left, too, and walked with the crowd to a church, attended Mass, walked up to the altar and had holy ash smeared on our foreheads.

It was Ash Wednesday. The forty-day mourning period of Lent had begun. The joyous, pre-Lenten, Carnival was over. The Red and Black revellers looked suitably sombre.

At the back of their minds, however, as in ours, glowed the thought that another year lay ahead and so, happily, did another, bubbling, Goan Carnival.

The Xavierian Imperative

VELHA GOA

It's a continuing miracle.

He died five centuries ago. His body was buried in an island in China without embalming or refrigeration or the use of any preservatives. Two years later, in 1554, his body was exhumed and received in triumph in Goa. It now lies in a glass coffin. The flesh has not decomposed, though recently, the skin has shown signs of wrinkling. There is no scientific explanation for

The tomb of the naturally preserved body of St. Francis Xavier.

Traditionally, Iberian altars used carved and gilded wood.

the natural preservation of his body. And if there is no scientific explanation for an event then it is called a miracle. The body so preserved is that of St. Francis Xavier. It lies in a church in a township of churches, monasteries and convents called Velha Goa or Old Goa: a place that lives both in the present and also in the distant, unchanging, past.

We last visited Old Goa on a warm, humid day. Along with us there were hundreds of other tourists clicking their cameras and mobile phones, mopping their brows, clustering around their guides who spouted their spiels in seven different languages. We had switched on our recorder to tape our comments when a snappy Goan guide began speaking to a group of South African visitors, including many of Indian origin from Durban: "Back in the 16th century, this was the capital of the Portuguese colony in India. Imagine it, folks. Down that road a *fidalgo*, a noble warrior, comes trotting on his spirited, caparisoned, horse, plumes in his hat, sword at his side. And he stops, right there, throws his reins to his servant, sweeps off his hat, and bows low as a beautiful lady descends from her coach drawn by four black horses. The *fidalgo* is probably her gallant, her companion as some would call him today. Goa, this place was called only Goa then, was a very licentious capital in those days. Most married women had a boyfriend on the side who showered them with gifts. See the diamonds glittering on her bosom, smell the fragrance of the perfume with which her maids had drenched her body, note the high platforms on her shoes that make it difficult for her to walk without the assistance of her servants. Observe the priest hurrying out of the church to greet the great woman with her multiple surnames as befits nobility. Also get a whiff of the open drains. Oof! The Portuguese had to abandon Old Goa as their capital because it became so unhygienic. They moved to Panjim where the sea breezes blew in from the Arabian Sea, and the flowing Mandovi kept the sewers flushed..."

He had, very accurately, described Old Goa as it had been in the 16th century.

We moved away and decided to walk around Old Goa.

Virtually all the secular buildings have gone, abandoned when the capital moved to Panjim, now known as Panaji. The government in Portugal's Lisbon had got worried about the growing power of Goa: at that time it had more inhabitants than London, more wealth than Antwerp. Besides, even the Pope in Rome had felt threatened by the growing might of the Church in Goa and the Vatican had banned some of its stronger priestly associations. All this led to the decline of the civic constructions in Old Goa and so, in course of time, they crumbled and fell under the onslaught of the drenching monsoons. Only the churches, convents and monasteries remained because the priests and nuns looked after them.

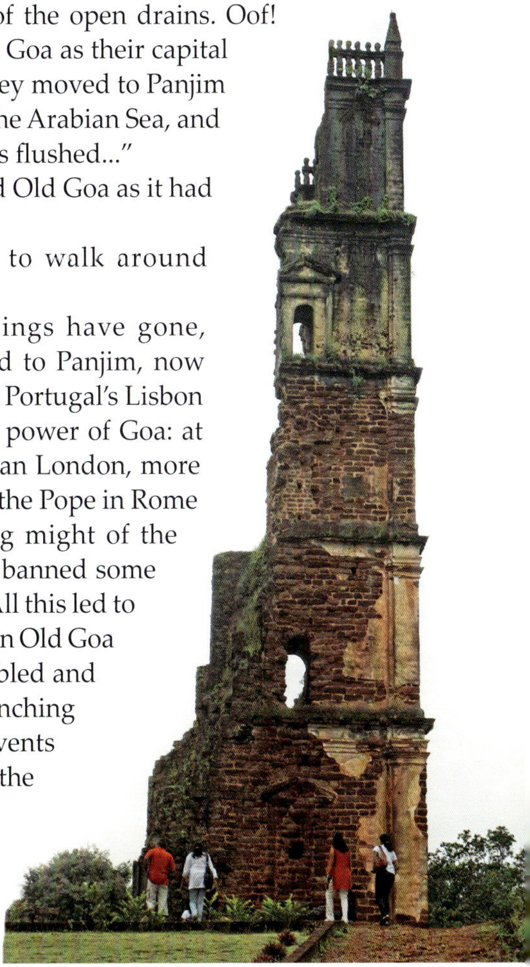

The 46-metre belfry of the Church of St. Augustine.

Left: The impressive Viceroy's Arch.
Below: Se Cathedral with its bell tower.

We ambled down the shaded roads, saw the old Viceroy's Arch through which the Portuguese governors had made their ceremonial entrance into Goa when today's Velha Goa was the only Goa.

We strode up to the oldest existing church in Old Goa: the Church of Our Lady of the Rosary. It's a very simple church built like a fortress and one of the few in the Manueline style: windows high on the roof-line and some typical architectural motifs in the rope-and-shell design. It crowns an escarpment and we walked to the edge and looked down. Below us the Mandovi flowed, brown and powerful. Beyond were the islands of Divar and Chorao. To the left, that is to the west, spread the glistening lowlands of Panaji. On the 25th of November, 1510, Alfonso de Albuquerque stood here and saw his army defeat that of Adil Shah. This church was built to commemorate that victory.

But for all their proclaimed devotion to their faith, and its strict code of conduct, the powerful Portuguese nobles and traders had their own views

A statue of Vasco da Gama in the Viceroy's Arch.

on morality. Inside the church is a memorial to the first Portuguese woman to arrive in Goa. Her name was Dona Caterina a Piro and she was the great and good friend of Governor Garcia da Sa. Saint Francis Xavier was shocked to find that though they had lived together for many years they were not married. He managed to persuade them to take their marital vows when Dona Caterina was on her deathbed.

St. Francis must have been a thorn in the side of the libidinous gentry of Goa but they admired his courage so much that they made him the patron saint of their colony. In many ways he continues to nurture Goa, particularly Old Goa. Every year thousands of pilgrims and tourists visit this religious township which, in turn, has led to the preservation of these Portuguese-era buildings and earned for them the status of a World Heritage Site recognised by the UNESCO.

As we always do, we said a prayer in the great old Se Cathedral with its superbly toned bell. Catholic tradition required all work to stop when the bell tolled at midday for the Angelus prayer. This, in Goa, also marked the formal lunch break. When, however, the priests in the Se Cathedral learnt that some employers did not allow their workers to rest till the last peal of the bell, they took to ringing the great bell half-an-hour earlier.

Left: The great altar of Bom Jesus.
Below: The Basilica of Bom Jesus.

We were not there at midday so we don't know if this tradition is still being followed in letter and spirit.

Most of the important churches of Old Goa are clustered around the Se because that was the official seat of the local head of the Catholic religion. The Se, however, is not the most important church in Old Goa today. Across the road from it rises the impressive, laterite, Church of Bom Jesus now elevated to the status of a Basilica principally because it holds the body of St. Xavier.

Whenever we have entered this church, we have always been struck by the main altar at the far end of the nave. Its intricately carved wood has been gilded. The altar is dominated by a statue of St. Ignatius Loyala. He was a Spanish officer who was wounded in battle, and was a friend of St. Xavier. The two friends teamed up with a third and formed the Society of Jesus (s.j.), a powerful teaching order of

Hindu artisans seemed to have influenced the internal structure of St. Catejan's Church.

priests known as the Jesuits. They have made St. Xavier's into a virtual brand image for excellence in education.

In keeping with the Jesuits' obsession with perfection, Bom Jesus is a superb example of the resplendence of the baroque style of art. It was all the rage when the church was built though it is often considered too ornate for modern minimalist tastes. But the sense of reverence in this church tones down the impact of its decorations. Much of this feeling of religious awe is centred on a side altar which is, really, a tomb. It was given by the Duke of Tuscany and created by the Florentine sculptor Giovanni Batista Foggini. He took ten years to complete it in jasper, marble and bronze. On top of it

lies the casket holding the body of St. Francis Xavier. It has glass panels on its sides and has been opened many times for the public to pay their respects to the Patron Saint of Goa.

We had left the church when we saw the South African tourists trooping in behind their guide. We turned round and followed them because we wanted to hear what the guide would say about the body. This time he kept strictly to the historical facts without using his imagination to conjure up the past. When he had finished, however, a woman in a floppy hat asked, "Is it true that once, when the body was exposed for veneration, a woman bit off its toe and she was caught because a trail of blood was left by the severed toe?" The guide looked at her, shaking his head ruefully. Then he said: "Madam, there is no need to create myths when there is a miracle, here, before your very eyes!"

As we said, someone, in the future, might give a scientific explanation for the uncorrupted body of St. Francis Xavier. But until that is done, it will remain a visible miracle.

Above: The Italianesque Church of St. Cajetan. Left: A statue of St. Francis Xavier stands between sinuous pillars.

About the Authors

Hugh and Colleen Gantzer live their dream. Colleen had always wanted to fly and she did pilot a plane in the Swiss Alps while Hugh sat behind saying a rosary, just in case! Hugh had longed to see those faraway places with their strange sounding names so he joined the Indian Navy. Hugh took premature retirement when he was the Judge Advocate of the Southern Naval Area and Hugh and Colleen decided to become a travel-writer-photographer team.

Suddenly, things changed. They found themselves surfing on the great travel wave that was sweeping across the world. In quick succession they launched India's first travel column carried in all editions of a national daily on the editorial page. They hosted fifty-two weekly episodes of India's first nation-wide TV travel show, wrote the first travel scripts for dot.coms, won national and international awards, toured India and the world as guests of eager tourism organisations. They have, possibly, visited, photographed and written about more places in India than anyone else in the long history of our land.

Once, a greatly revered maternal uncle, who had just retired as India's Naval Chief, had asked them, "How long more will you continue to travel?" That was before they were invited to a winter ball in Vienna. Today, for six months every year, when they're not in their Victorian cottage in the oak woods of the Himalayas, they're still travelling...and they're still having a ball.

Other Books in the Intriguing India Series

The Alluring *North*

The Colourful *East*

The Historic *South*